JN409285

The 33rd Great Prize of The World Poetry(2019)

Winner 수상자 : Poet Kim Jeong-won 김정원 시인

* Graduated from English Dept. of Yonsei University, and from a graduate School of Education in Yonsei University, and from a graduate School of Myongji Univetsity
* Made first Debut as a Poet in The Literature Monthly.
* Collection(Anthology) of Poems:<Washing cold Hands>, <Pilgrim of Time>, <You were a Flower in other Heaven>, <Place of Emptiness>, <The late Autumn's Sunlight is very Warm>, The Anthology, <The life's Fin>, <The Alter Ego> tr. by Won Eung-Soon in Korean-English>, and <A Group Counselling, tr, by Kim Jeong-Won>, etc.
* Served as a Lecturer at Seongkyunkwn University and Myeongji University
* Won a Prize of Yulmok Literature, of Race Litetature, of Sowol Literature
* Member of Korea Pen in International, and Korea Writer's Association of Society of the Mirae Poets, Member of the Christian Writer;s Association of Korea, Director of Society of Female Literature of Korea
* E-mail: wooajnee@hanmail.net

* 연세대학교 영문과 졸업, 동 교육대학원 및 명지대학원 졸업
* 〈월간문학〉 신인상 당선으로 문단에 오름
* 시집으로 〈시인 손을 닦으며〉, 〈시간의 순례〉, 〈다른 하늘에서도 넌 꽃이었느니〉,〈허虛의 자리〉, 〈늦가을 햇살이 참 따뜻하구나〉, 〈삶의 지느러미〉,
* 한영대역시집 〈분신〉 (원응순 역), 본인 번역서로 〈집단 카운슬링〉이 있음.
* 성균관대학교와 명지대학교 강사 역임
* 수상: 율목문학상, 민족문학상, 소월문학상
* 국제펜 한국본부 회원, 한국문인협회 회원, 한국여성문학인회 이사, 미래시인회 회원, 한국크리스천문학가협회 회원

A Wall Clock

A clock was looking down on us
At the night when your white hairs
Glistened unusually.

I looked at the clock,
f you were not there, we should be young, still.

The short(hour) hand walked briskly
The long hand followed it with light strides
Carrying the sun and moon again,
Mopping its sweat
Like man and wife(a couple) living day by day.

Ticking, ticking
They managed lives harmoniously
Very earnestly orderly
They devote themselves to a task,
The serving minds are good to look.

Ticking, ticking,
A secret talk lf mutability!

벽시계

벽시계가 우릴 내려다보고 있었다
당신의 흰 머리카락이
유난히 반짝이던 밤

나는 시계를 쳐다보고
"자네가 없었으면 우린 아직 젊을 텐데"

시침(時針)이 성큼성큼 걸어갔다
분침이 총총걸음으로 따라갔다
해와 달을 치켜 업으며
구슬땀 닦으며
나날에 살아가는 부부같이

똑딱똑딱
사이좋게 목숨을 경영했다
참 질서 있게 열심히
생업에 종사하는구나
봉헌하는 순정이 참 보기 좋다

똑딱똑딱
무상의 밀어(密語)여.

■ **Evaluation**

Excellent Poems Sublimating our Life's Sufferings as Dream's 'Operation'

The poetic attitude of Kim Jeong-won's <The Wall Clock>, is more closer to the reverence than a poor excavation about life or reception. To substitute, to devote, and manage objects that are perceived through the poet's eyes as "you", the poet's endurance to life seems to be healthy, but the poet's poetical techniques expressing it as "consecration" is a startled humor supporting the whole poems.

So are the same cases, such a hypocrisy willing 'to vanish as an eraser' or 'a sadness like fine texture' to spread as 'an umbrella' showing in other poem, <An Echo of the Mountain> and <A Pine Tree on the Cliff>.

The poet's poems show us to brush and stroke our life 'making our life shine unusually'. And they make us aware that even the karma effects, 'carrying the sun and the moon on our back' are the big pacification of our life.

I really wish that this poetic achievement would be dedicated to the finality of the poet's life getting ahead to walk on briskly.

- Judges: Won Eung-soon, O Jin-hwan, Gwon O-un)

■ 심사평

삶의 곤고함을 꿈의 '경영' 으로 승화시킨 수작

김정원의 〈벽시계〉의 시적 태도는, 삶에 대한 섣부른 천착이나 수용(受容)이기보다는 경외감에 더 가까이 가 있는 듯하다. '내려다보는' 대상을 '자네'로 환치시킨다거나, '종사' 하고 '경영' 하는 것으로 보아 삶의 부지(扶持)가 분명해 보이는 데도 그것을 '봉헌' 으로 치부하는 기법은 그의 전편을 떠받치는 섬뜩한 골계(滑稽)다.

그의 다른 작품 〈산의 울림〉에서 보이는 '지우개로 소멸' 되고 싶다는 위악이나, '세모시 같은 비애' 를 '우산' 으로 펴 드는 (〈벼랑의 소나무〉) 경우들이 그 예다.

이처럼 김정원의 시는 삶을 '유난히 반짝이도록' 닦고 쓰다듬는다. 또 '해와 달은 업고' 가는 업보마저도 삶의 커다란 위무임을 새삼 일깨우고 있다.

아무쪼록 오늘의 그의 시적 성취가 성큼성큼 앞서가는 그의 삶의 궁극에 이바지하기를 바라 마지않는다.

– 심사위원: 원응순, 오진환, 권오운(글)

The 33rd Main Prize of The World Poetry(2019)

Winner 수상자 : Poet Jung Hyun-im 정현임 시인

* Poet and Artist(Painter).

* Director of the Society of the World Poetry.

* Literary Man's Association of the Korea Race Literature.

* Awarding Prizes: Won the Main Prize of the Korea Race Literature.
Won the Special Prize of Public Subscription for the Korea Woman's Fine Arts.

* Poetical Works: "A Small Island of the Afternoon", "I Won't Lament Any More", "I Would Like To Say 'Love You'", "A Little Dream As Being One"

* Address: #20(3rd Story), Unchi-ro No.100 gil, Buk-gu, Gwangju City, Korea.

* Mobile : 010-5642-7923

* E-mail: hyeonim9282@daum.net

* 월간 문예사조 2001년 시 부문 신인상

* 현재 시인이며 화가로 활동

* 세계시문학회 이사

* 한국민족문학가협회 회원

*수상 : 한국민족문학상 본상
한국여성미술공모전 특별상 외

*시집 : 『오후의 작은 섬』
『난 더 이상 슬퍼하지 않을 거야』
『사랑한다고 말하고 싶었는데』
『작은 꿈 하나 되어』

*E-mail : hyeonim9282@daum.net

To Sprout a Little Dream

I budded one little dream
Seeming to pass, or to forget
After the time by the mind's anchor,
And my breast was moved
By one dream at childhood,
Flashing across my mind unexpectedly.

Not to lose you(dream),
Every time when my mind was delicate,
Taking out a little dream one by one to look,
You and I are united as one endlessly.

Though having unsatisfied feelings yet,
Compared to realizing all things,
The hours, flowing on after my mind
Sit together,
And sprout a little dream. again.

작은 꿈 하나 되어

작은 꿈 하나 싹을 틔웠지
마음의 닻으로 시간 따라 흐르며
잊은 듯하다가
문득 문득 떠오르는
그 어릴 적 꿈 하나로
내 가슴은 흔들렸었지

너를 놓칠 수 없었기에
마음이 애잔해 질 때마다
작은 꿈 하나씩 꺼내어 바라보며
너와 나는 끝없이 하나가 되었지.

다 이루었다 하기엔
아직도 미진하지만
여기 이 자리,
나의 마음 따라 흘러온 시간들이
한데 모여 앉아
작은 꿈 다시 싹 틔워 보네

■ Evaluation

Another Dream of the Poet, 'Sprouted one little Dream'

Dream should be sprouted before it dreams. Because it makes a process intercept originally being lost in a simple daydream. A dream's bud(germ) is so callous and solid that it is apt to appear as a fancy like a cold fish or a phantom.

The poet, Jung Hyun-im's all poems including <Becoming one little Dream> are based on talking back as a naked face. Ordinally speaking,

in dedicating greatly to a life as an alive thing to sprout, this poet's poems have the reason for their being.

So this poet has lots of dreams. The province of the poet's dream has many kinds, and very specialty. The dream's bundle is filled with '<Becoming one little Dream> which the poet at any time can bring out', and with '<One Dream> to vanish or to scatter', and at the same time, <My Dream> falling down from the Galaxy communicates secretly with shooting stars(meteors).

Now this poet should solve the problem which the landslide of the poet's dream should not appear as a simple fancy. Therefore I think, it is also a share for the poet to serve other dream's route for a long time.

- Judges: Won Eung-soon, O Jin-hwan, Gwon O-un

■ 심사평

'작은 꿈 하나 싹을 틔운' 시인의 또 하나의 꿈

꿈은 이루어지기 전에 싹을 틔워야 하나 보다. 그것이 단순한 몽상으로 떨어지는 것을 근원적으로 차단하는 과정이 되는 까닭이다. 꿈의 싹은 야무지고 옹골차서 생파리 같은 환영이나 곡두의 모습으로 나타나기 일쑤이다.

〈작은 꿈 하나 되어〉를 비롯한 정현임의 모든 시편들이 민낯으로 대거리를 할 수 있는 기반이 되는 것도 이에 근거한다. 좀 더 범박하게 말하면, 꿈은 싹을 틔우는 생체로서 삶에 크게 기여하는데 정현임이 이에 철저하게 덧붙이고 있다.

그래서 그의 꿈은 참으로 많다. 그의 꿈의 영역은 따라서 다양하고 뚝별나다. 그의 꿈보따리는 수시로 '꺼내 볼 수 있는 (〈작은 꿈 하나 되어〉)' 꿈들로 가득하다. 또 '사라지고 흩어져 버릴(〈꿈 하나〉)' 그것들로 가득하고, '은하에서 떨어져 내리는 (〈나의 꿈은〉)' 유성과도 긴밀히 내통한다.

이제 이런 그의 꿈의 사태(沙汰)가 한낱 허상으로 떨어지지 않아야 하는 과제를 풀어야 한다. 꿈에서 깨어나 오래도록 또 다른 꿈길에 이바지해야 하는 것 또한 온전히 그의 몫이다.

－심사위원: 원응순, 오진환, 권오운(글)

The 33rd Main Prize of The World Poetry(2019)

Winner 수상자 : Poet Yoon Hyoung-soon 윤형순 시인

* Pen Name: Woojeon
* Born at Gangjin, Jeonna-namdo, Korea
* Graduated from College of Agriculture, Jeon-Nam University
* Served at Ministry office of Agriculture for 35Years, and at National Agricultural Co-operation Federation.
* Received the Prize in Literary Contest for Poetry under the Auspices of Jeonnam Daily Newspaer(1965)
* Manager of the Kindred Society of the Haenam Family "Yun"(2012)
* The Prize of the Public Officer(1985)
* The Prize of the Proud Officer for the National Agricultural Assocition (1989)
* Member of the World Poetry Institute
*Poetic Anthology: "Homesickness"

* 아호 우전(牛田)
* 전남 강진 출생
* 강진중 · 농고 졸업
* 전남대학교 농과대학 졸업
* 농수산부와 농협중앙회(35년 근무)
* 모범공무원상 수상(1985)
* 자랑스런 농협인상 수상(1989)
* 해남 윤씨 중앙종친회 자문위원
* (사) 행당윤복선생기념사업회본부장 (2012)
* 전남일보 후원 시창작컨테스트에서 수상(1965)
* 세계시문학회 회원
* 시집 : 『향수(鄕愁)』

The Path Going to You

When a forest is careless
The path is in sight.
On my sad path in the yellow soil colored
For a home town,

A warbler cries
So as for my finger tips to tremble.
When a dazzling sky of my hometown
Enters your mind,
The wood is careless
The path going to you
Comes in sight.

The wood is to be careless
For you to be visible.

너에게 가는 길

숲이 무심할 때
길이 보이더라
황톳빛 서러운
고향 길에서

살끝이 시리도록
꾀꼬리 울더라
눈시린
고향 하늘이
가슴에 와 있을 때
숲은 무심하고
너에게 가는 길이 보이더라

숲이 무심해야
네가 보이더라.

제33회 세계시문학 본상(2019)_ 윤형순

■ Evaluation

The Poet Stands between the Two Ways of Poetry

Crossing over a river side/ A path for the corn field
A wayfarer/ as the moon flows on the clouds

About the above the famous poem, <A Wayfarer> by Park Mok-wol, the poet, Seo Jung-joo(Midang) had written a critical appreciation in his critical essay of poetry <The Modern Poetry of Korea> like this:

In a word, the distinctive feature of this poetry has a strong point expressing sentiments on his unique native place, specially on the good emotions of the southern province.

The poet, Yoon Hyoung-soon's poem <The Way Going To You> is emitting much fragrance of his southern native place. No, adding to this, he poet, Han Ha-wun's sentiment as 'sorrowful as colors of the native earth', this poetic clause even 'makes our hand's tip smart'.

In the sheer cliff there are two ways, one way is called such a way as 'Andolit-Gil' turning round the rock in one's arms, and the other way as 'Jidolit-Gil' turning round the rock on one's back'. So is the way of his poetry, 'The morning sunbeams caressing a port, Gugang-Po' in <A Gumgok Temple> is the former way, the poem, <Solitude> is the latter way, which we promote a lonesome feeling to calm down a solitude.

Which way is the poet's way, I think, the poet Yoon Hyoung-soon's poetical technique to handle poems can be guaranteed with safety.

- Judges: Won Eung-soon, O Jin-hwan, Gwon O-un)

■ 심사평

시의 길에도 안돌잇길이 있고 지돌잇길이 있나니

강나루 건너서/ 밀밭길을 // 구름에 달 가듯이/ 가는 나그네

박목월의 이 〈나그네〉에 대해, 미당(未堂)은 그의 시론집 ≪한국의 현대시≫에서 다음과 같은 감상을 술회한 적이 있다.

'그의 시의 특색은 한마디로, 우리 고유의 향토정서를 소재로 한 것 가운데, 특히 남방적 향토정서를 표현하는 장점이 있다.'

윤형순의 〈너에게 가는 길〉도, 남방적 향토정서가 물씬한 작품이다. 아니 거기다 '황토빛 서러운' 한하운(韓何雲) 정서까지 덧붙여져서 그야말로 '살끝이 시려' 온다.

삶의 벼랑에는, 바위를 안고 돌아가는 안돌잇길도 있고, 바위를 등에 대고 돌아가는 지돌잇길도 있다. 시의 길도 그러하거늘, '구강포를 어루만지는 아침 햇살(〈금곡사〉)이 그 앞이요, ' 외로움을 달래기 위해 외로움을 키우는 '(〈고독〉) 것이 뒤엣것이라 할 수 있다.

윤형순의 시의 길이 어느 편이든 시를 조물락거리는 기술은 확보되어 있는 것 같아 마음 놓인다.

－심사위원 : 원응순, 오진환, 권오운(글)

The 32nd Prize of the World Poetry Literature Awarding Ceremony
Commemoration Ceremony For Publication of The 36th Series of World Poetry

- 일시 : 2018년 11월 23일(금) 오후 5시
- 장소 : 마포구 합정동주민센터 3층
- 主催 : 世界詩文學會 • 後援 : 을지출판공사 · 한국수력원자력(주) 한빛원자력본부

국민의례

인사말을 하는 세계시문학회 원응순 회장

경과보고를 하는 세계시문학회 신동명 부회장

심사보고를 하는 김지원 심사위원장

축사를 하는 유승우 현대시협 이사장 (전)

축사를 하는 손해일 국제펜 한국본부 이사장

축사를 하는 홍춘표 구로문협 명예회장

세계시문학상 대상

홍 윤 표 시인

세계시문학상 본상

전 홍 구 시인

The B-Cup Show Window at Sangdo-dong 상도

마포구 합정동주민센터 3층

을지출판공사, 한국수력원자력(주) 한빛원자력본

1부 진행 : 윤수아 세계시문학회 사무국장

2부 진행 : 오진환 세계시문학회 부회장

시낭송을 하는 장동석 시인

시낭송을 하는 강영덕 시인

시낭송을 하는 정현임 시인

시낭송을 하는 남창희 시인

시낭송을 하는 윤형순 시인

시낭송을 하는 형정희 시인

세계시문학 사화집 봉정 후

제38차 정기총회

■ 일시 : 2019년 2월 19일 (화) ■ 장소 : 서울 합정동 들풀

임원회의

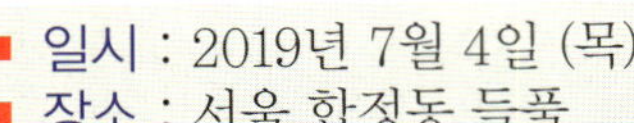

■ 일시 : 2019년 7월 4일 (목)
■ 장소 : 서울 합정동 들풀

회장 이 · 취임식 및 임원 · 이사 위촉식

■ 일시 : 2019년 3월 26일 (화) ■ 장소 : 서울 합정동 들풀

문학회 회장 이 · 취임
19년 임원 이사 위촉식
원응순 오진환
3. 26(화) 4시

문학회
19년 임원 위촉식
원응순 오진환

취임식
원 및 이사 위촉식
축

019년 임원 및 이사 위촉

문학회 회장 이 · 취임
19년 임원 이사 위촉식
원응순 오진환
3. 26(화) 4시

원응순이임, 6대 오진환
26(화) 4시

회장 이 · 취임식
축
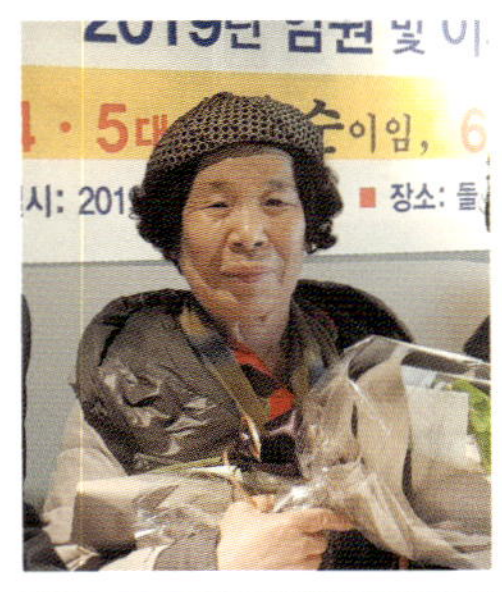
2019년 임원 및
순이임,

학회 회장 이 · 취임
임원 위촉식
응순이임, 오진환

및 이사 위촉식
축

회장 이 · 취임식
원 및 이사 위촉식
축

취임식
환취임

순이임, 오진환취임
합정역 5번출

회장
임식

9년 임원 및 이사 위촉식
26(화) 4시

회장 이 · 취임식
원 및 이사
장소: 들 풀

임원 및 이사 위촉식
순이임 진환취임
4시

9년 임원 및 이사
26(화) 4시

회 회장 이 · 취임식
임원 및 위촉식
순이임, 진환취임

2019 봄 문학기행

■ 일시 : 2019년 4월 23일 (화) ■ 장소 : 강원도 양구 두타연 · 평화의댐

2019 라오스 해외 문학 연수

■ 일시 : 2019년 6월 3일~7일 ■ 장소 : 동독국립대학교·비엔티안·방비엥

2019 시낭송

■ 일시 : 2019년 9월 24일 (화)
■ 장소 : 서울 인사동 시가연

2019 가을 문학기행

■ 일시 : 2019년 10월 24일 (목) ■ 장소 : 충북 증평 소월 · 경암문학기념관

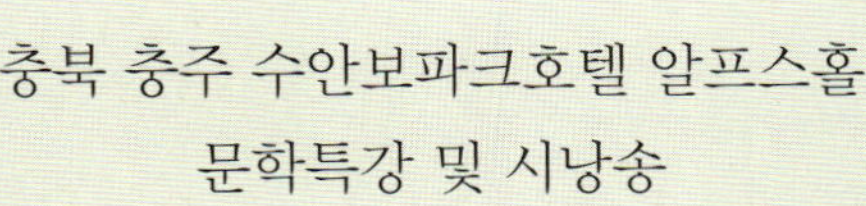

충북 충주 수안보파크호텔 알프스홀
문학특강 및 시낭송

Poems of Kim Jeong-won

김정원 시집

The Alter Ego

분신

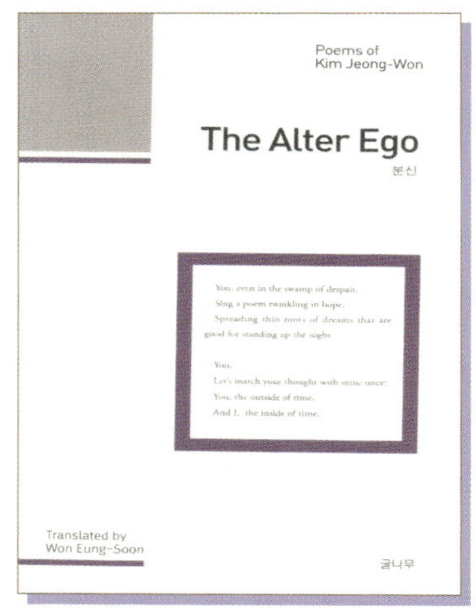

세월 따라 인간의 삶을 차차 허무하게 이해해 가는
아픔들이 진해지면서 밝은 무대를 점점 어둡게 비춘다.
그러나 슬픈 노래로 슬픔을 치유할 수도 있지 않을까?

–시인의 말 중에서

정현임 시집

작은 꿈 하나 되어

이 시집은 내 삶 중 가장 어려운 고비에 쓰여졌다.
나약한 의지를 지키려는 몸부림의 일상
고요와 적막에서 오는 두려움
아랑곳없이 피어나는 꽃들의 아름다운 슬픔
그리고 애써 스스로를 가둬 버린 시간들
글로, 말로는 다 표현할 수 없는 약속들이
어쩌면 지켜질 수 없다는 약속이란 걸
이 글을 쓰며 배웠다.
나에게는 이 시집이 징검다리가 되어서
내가 다시 세상과 소통하는 계기가 되길 소망한다.

—「시인의 말」 중에서

윤형순 시집

鄕 愁

윤형순 시인은 고향을 떠나 외지생활을 하는 동안 사회적으로 출세하고, 인간적으로 성공한 우리 세대의 모델로, 그의 경지가 너무 멀고 높아서 근접할 수 없는 처지이며 학처럼 고아하고, 내면에 잠재된 유토피아를 외면하지 않는 인격의 소유자이다.

—양치중 시인의 발문에서

내 가노라 저 멀리/뭉게구름 수평선 너머/초승달 드리운 조각배에/밤하늘 별빛 동무 삼아//신장로 한복판에 희미한 달그림자/구름 사이 얼굴 내밀고/새소리도 대나무숲에 숨죽이며/한가족 모여 살고//황량한 칼바람 머리 위에/성난 야수의 몸부림/광야에 드리운 달그림자//우물 속에 떠 있는 표주박/조각배 되어/고향 하늘로. – 〈鄕愁〉 전문

세계시문학 37집 발간을 축하합니다

오진환 시집

산은 구름을 탓하지 않는다

시를 통해 성장시킨 내 삶의 길에서
탐구하며 걸었던 교육자의 길 35년,
건강한 웃음으로 행복을 추구하며
시를 통해 나의 인생을
더욱 성장시키려고 노력했습니다.
부끄러운 마음으로
시집을 상재함을
주님께 영광돌립니다.

신동명 시집

새 벽 달

'산 안에 산이 잠들어 있는' 경우만큼 먹먹한 때가 다시 또 있으랴 싶다. 그런데도 시인은 '보지 않아도 보이고, 듣지 않아도 들린다'며 깊은 꿈에 든 겨울산의 처연한 음성으로 노닥거린다. 그 끈덕진 노닥거림이 바로 신동명 시의 근골이 된다. 허옇게 뿜어 올리는 근골의 입김이 된다.

– 권오운 시인의 「해설」 중에서

세계시문학 37집 발간을 축하합니다

이상진 이야기 I

역사와 함께
미래를 생각하다

"사람의 일생은 무거운 짐을 지고 먼 길을 가는 것과 같다. 서두르지 말라."라는
인생훈을 반복하면서 "역사는 이상의 현실화 과정이며 역사의 신은 반드시 승리한다."는
명제 앞에 겸손함과 경건함을 다짐합니다. (자서 중에서)

맹숙영 시집

아름다운 비밀

아름다운 비밀이 암시하고 있는
것처럼 시의 경향에 앞서
그의 언어들이
꾸밈없는 시심에서 그려졌을 때
가능해진 까닭입니다.

– 이인평 시인의 서평 중에서

세계시문학 37집 발간을 축하합니다

박윤기 시집

낙동강의 노을

부끄러운 마음으로 원고를 넘겨주고 가만히 지나온 세월의 무게를 느껴 봅니다.
어린 시절 꿈만 안고 구름 속을 헤매는 달과 같이, 산천을 헤매는 바람같이 떠돌아다닌 시간들을 이제야 되짚어 봅니다.
낙동강변 임경대에 가서 막걸리 한 잔에 고향 안부를 묻고 싶습니다. –시인의 말 중에서

이람 구명숙 시집

뭉클

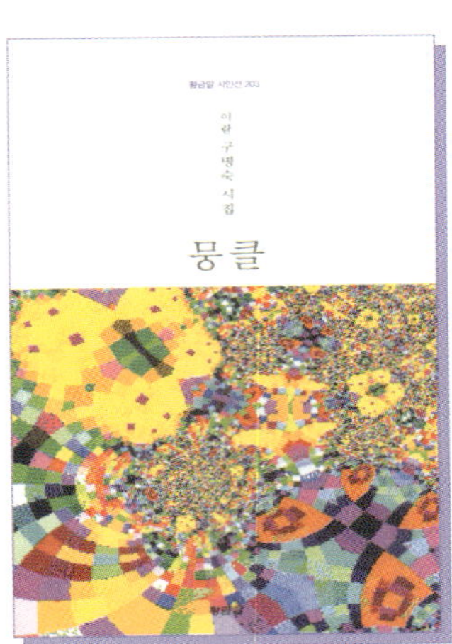

심미적 사유와 감각의 세계를
완결한 이번 시집의 성취를 넘어,
구명숙 시인은
또 다른 넓은 세계로 한 걸음 더
나아가고 있음을 봅니다.

(유성호 문학평론가)

세계시문학 37집 발간을 축하합니다

하나로 선

사상과 문학

한국문단과 세계문단의
미래를 이끌어 갈
참신하고 역량 있는
신인 작가를 발굴하여
문학의 새 지평을 열어가는
문학지.
하나로 선 사상과 문학은
늘 여러분과 함께합니다.

윤 자 시집

꽃씨 뿌리듯 시를 짓네

철마다 피는 꽃처럼
내 마음에도
꽃 피고
꽃씨 뿌리듯
시를 짓네

나는
큰 들의 딸이라네.

–『꽃씨 뿌리듯 시를 짓네』 일부

World Poetry

世界詩文學 세계시문학

Vol.37/2019

EDITOR : OH JIN-HWAN

조기현 작「하늘과 바다의 연정」

EulJi Publishing Company
을지출판공사
Republic of Korea

WORLD POETRY 世界詩文學 세계시문학
Vol.37 / 2019
(price; $20)

EDITOR : Oh Jin-hwan

Published by : Kim Hyo-yeol / 김효열
EulJi Publishing Company 을지출판공사
〈등록번호 제 2-741호 1985. 2. 14 등록〉
41, Yanghwajin-gil, Mapo-go, Seoul, Korea
TEL (02) 334-4050 FAX (02) 334-4010
e-mail : ejp4050@hanmail.net

Pubilshed on November 27, 2019. Printed on November 20, 2019

The Society of the World Poetry
#603. 41, Yanghwajin-gil, Mapo-go, Seoul, Korea
e-mail : wp1982@hanmail.net
Tel. 82-2-334-4050 Mobile 82-10-2324-3454, 82-10-5291-5522

CONTENTS

England

France

Germany

Greece

India

Italia

Japan

Korea

Peru

Portugal

Spain

Sweden

U.S.A

***A Preface**

The World Poetry Soaring Up "Toward World and Future"

Oh Jin-hwan
President of the World Poetry

Dear Members of the World Poetry, and our Honorable Guests of Literature, home and abroad!

I am the poet, O Jin-hwan, elected newly as the 6th president of the society of the World Poetry in the general assembly in March, 2019. Our society of the World Poetry was founded in November 26, 1982, along with the high and grand aims of studying a new poetics and the poet's international exchanges of culture for a literary emotion and human intelligence.

The first enforcement of King system in Korea was done at Gaya country in A.D. 42, at that period Soo-ro Kim was a King with a gold crown. We formulated a law conferring a prize on a winner recognized as a great poet in remembrance of the King's gold crown every year. So I am very sensible of heavy responsibility as a chairman of the world poetry.

Our literary society now has the history of 37years, publishing 37volumes of the poetic anthology, and also produced the 80 great poets throughout the world

Now we are living here at the age that AI is controlling human emotional and intelligent realm. This situations all human beings faced are not good, disillusioned a little, but we have to keep trying to create the highest poems holding a life's rope named 'hope', expecting that our members would take the lead in writing good works to provoke our internal changes.

Today, specially I would like to congratulate next three prize winners, clapping the great prize winner, the poet Kim Jeong-won, the main prize, the poet Jung Hyun-im, and the main prize, the poet Yoon Hyoung-soon, and I would like to be very grateful to judges, who tried to examine their poems minutely, also together to our members who were willing to submit their manuscripts and to make a donation for our world poetry.

Thanks very much.

Nov. 27, 2019.

■ 권두언

"세계로 미래로" 비상하는 World Poetry

세계시문학회 회장 오 진 환

친애하는 세계시문학회 회원여러분, 그리고 내외 귀빈 여러분!

2019년 세계시문학회 총회에서 제6대 회장으로 선출된 오진환 시인입니다. 세계시문학회는 1982년 11월 26일 창립되었습니다. 세계시문학회는 시문학을 연구하며 세계적인 문화 정서와 인간 지성을 위한 시인들의 국제적 교류를 목적으로 창립하였습니다.

그 후 한국 최초의 왕 제도가 시행된 AD 42년 가야국 김수로왕이 착관한 가야금관왕관상을 세계시문학상으로 제정, 시행하여 세계 저명한 시인들에게 시상케 되었습니다. 이런 단체의 회장직을 맡게 되니 어깨가 무겁습니다.

창립 이후 많은 세계의 시인들이 시의 교류를 통하여 문화 창달의 계기로 삼은 지 어언 37년이란 시간이 흘렀습니다. 세계시문학회 연혁이 말해 주듯이 연간 사화집 37집을 출간하였으며 지금까지 80여 명의 국내외 시인들이 수상의 영예를 안았습니다.

인공지능(AI)이 인간의 감성을 지배하는 시대에 우리는 살고 있습니다. 어느 영역까지 지배할지는 인간의 감성이 살아 있는 한 지켜볼 일이며 세계시문학회가 그 선두주자가 되기를 희망합니다.

第33회 세계시문학상 대상 수상자 김정원 시인, 본상 수상자 정현임 시인, 윤형순 시인께 축하와 영광을 드립니다.

심사를 맡아주신 심사위원님들께 감사드리고 작품을 제출해 주신 회원들에게도 고마움을 전합니다. 감사합니다.

2019. 11. 27

The General Prologue (from Canterbury Tales)

by Geoffrey Chaucer

  Whan that April with his showres soote
The droughte of March hath perced to the roote,
And bathed every veine in swich licour,
Of which vertu engendered is the flowr;
Whan Zephyrus eek with his sweete breeth
Inspired hath in every holt and heete
The tendre croppes, and the yonge sonne
Hath in the Ram his halve cours yronne,
And smale fowles maken melodye
That sleepen al the night with open ye−
That priketh hem Nature in hir corages−
Thanne longen folk to goon on pilgrimages,
And palmeres for to seeken stranunge strondes
To ferne halwes, couthe in sondry londes;
And specially from every shires ende.
Of Engelonde to Canterbury they wende,
The holy blisful martyr for to seeke
That hem hath holpen whan that they were seke.-

[Note] Geoffrey Chaucer(1340?~1400) : 존 드라이든(John Dryden)이 처음으로 쵸서를 영시의 아버지라고 부른 이래로 그대로 부름). 쵸서는 일찍이 궁전에 들어가 궁정인의 교양을 기르고, 프랑스의 “기욤드마쇼”와 “드샹”등을 읽고 프랑스시를 모방한 단시를 습작했으며 후에 “장미의 로망”이나 보에티우스의 “철학의 위안”를 번역한 역서 등이 있다. 위 시의 본문 등은 The Norton Anthology of English Literature를 참고했음.

서 시 (캔터베리 이야기의)

지오프리 쵸서 작/ 원응순 역주

4월의 감미로운 소나기가
3월의 가뭄을 속속들이 꿰뚫고
꽃을 피어나게 하는 습기로,
온 세상 나뭇가지의 힘줄을 적시어 주면
서녘바람 또한 달콤한 입김을
삼나무 밭 애송이 가지의 끝과 끝 속에 불어넣어 준다.
갓 시작한 태양은 백양궁의 반 여정을 마쳤을 뿐이며
작은 날짐승들은 저마다 노래를 부르고—
자연이 하도 그들의 가슴을 설레게 하여—
밤이면, 온통 뜬눈으로 잠을 잔도다.
사람들이 순례를 갈망하는 것은 이때,
성지순례자들은 낯선 나라들에 마음이 쏠리고, 먼 나라
고장마다 널리 칭송되는 여러 성인들의 묘소를 찾으려 한다.
특히 영국에서는 마을마다 앞을 다투어
캔터베리로 사람들이 몰려들어,
병들어 고생할 때, 그들을 도와준
거룩하고 복된 순교자를 찾아간다.

작품 "캔터베리 이야기": 12세기경, 영국의 왕, 헨리와 캔터베리 대주교 토마스 사이에 왕권과 교권(로마교회의 권력) 싸움에서 토마스 대주교가 캔터베리대성당 안에서 살해당한 (1170년) 사건 이래로 캔터베리는 일약 유명한 순례지가 되었다. 그리고 토마스는 성인(St. Thomas)이 되었다. "캔터베리 이야기"는 캔터베리로 순례 가는 30여명이 런던에서 그 곳 순례지 까지의 왕복 길에 한 순례자가 소개한 2개의 이야기를 모은 것이다. 이 작품은 그의 대표작으로 오히려 그의 "트로일러스와 크리세이드"(The Troilus and Chriseyde)를 능가하다는 평을 받고 있다.

—역주 원응순: 시인, 경희대 명예교수, 영문학 박사

Advice to A Prophet

by Richard Wilbur/ Tr. by Won Eung-soon

When you come, as you soon must, to the streets of our city,
Mad-eyed from stating the obvious,
Not proclaiming our fall but begging us
In God's name to have self-pity,

Spare us all word of the weapons, their force and range,
The long numbers that rocket the mind;
Out slow, unreckoning hearts will be left behind,
Unable to fear what is too strange.

Nor shall you scare us with talk of the death of the race.
How should we dream of this place without me?
The sun mere free, the leaves untroubled about us,
A stone look on the stone's face?

Speak of the world's own change. Though we cannot conceive
Of an undreamt thing, we know to our cost
How the dreamt cloud crumbles, the vines are blackened by frost,
How the view alters. We could believe,

If you told us so, that the white-tailed deer will slip
Into perfect shade, grown perfectly shy,
The lark avoid the reaches of our eye,

The jack-pine lose its knuckled grip

On the cold ledge, and every torrent burn
As Xanthus once, its gliding trout
Stunned in a twinkling. What should we be without
The dolphin's arc, the dove's return,

These things in which we have seen ourselves and spoken?
Ask us, prophet, how we shall call
Our natures forth when that live tongue is all
Dispelled, that glass obscured or broken

In which we have said the rose of our love and the clean
Horse of our courage, in which beheld
The singing locust of the soul unshelled,
And all we mean or wish to mean.

Ask us, ask us whether with the worldless rose
Our hearts shall fail us; come demanding
Whether there shall be lofty or long standing
When the bronze annals of the oak-tree close.

예언자에게 주는 충고

리처드 윌버/ 원 응 순 역주

당신이 조만간 우리도시에 오시어
명백한 사실을 말씀하시느라 눈에 광기를 띄우며,
우리의 멸망을 선언하는 대신에 제발
자기연민을 가지라고 하나님의 이름으로 간청하실 때,

무기와 그 파괴력과 사정거리와
마음을 뒤 흔드는 긴 숫자 이야기들은 참아 주십시오;
계산에 둔한 우리의 가슴은 너무 이상스러운 것을
두려워 할 줄 몰라 뒤에 처지게 될 것입니다.

또한 인류의 죽음에 대한 이야기로 우리에게 겁을 주지도 말아야 합니다.
어떻게 우리가 존재하지 않는 이곳을 꿈꿀 수가 있겠습니까?
태양은 다만 불덩이, 나무 잎들은 우리 주변에 조용한 채,
돌의 얼굴에는 돌의 모습만을 어떻게 상상할 수 있겠습니까?

세계 그 자체의 변화를 말씀하십시오, 꿈꾸어 보지 않은 것을
생각할 수는 없지만, 우리는 그럼에도 알고 있습니다,
어떻게 꿈같은 구름이 허물어지고 덩굴이 서리를 맞아 검게 되고,
풍경이 변하는 지를. 우리는 믿을 수 있습니다,

당신이 그처럼 말씀하신다면, 흰 꼬리 사슴이
몹시 수줍어져서 아주 그늘진 그늘 속으로 사라지고,

종달새는 우리의 눈을 벗어나고
벼랑의 차디찬 바위를 움켜쥐던 힘 있는 소나무가

떨어져 버리고, 옛날 잔터스 강처럼
한 때 모든 개울이 말라 버려 뛰놀던 송어들이
순식간에 기절해 버리는 사실들을. 우리가 어찌 되겠습니까,
만일 그 속에서 우리 자신들을 보고 말했던 돌고래의 공중묘기와,

비들기의 귀환이 없었다면?
예언자여, 물으십시오, 우리가 어떻게
우리의 인간성을 표현할 수 있겠는지를, 우리 사랑의
장미와 우리 용기라는 멋진 말[馬]을

말해주시던 살아있는 혀가 아주 없어져 버려
영혼의 노래하는 매미가 껍질을 벗고서
우리의 모든 의사와 뜻하는 사실을
비춰주던 그 거울이 흐려지거나 깨져 버릴 때에.

세계가 없는 장미로는 우리의 마음을
실망시키지 않겠느냐고 질문 하십시오; 혹은 참나무의
청동시기가 끝날 때에 그것이 계속 우람하고
오래토록 존속할 수 있을 것인지를 오셔서 캐물으십시오.

[해설과 낱말]

리처드 윌버(1921- ?)는 뉴욕 출신 시인으로, 1987년 미국 월계시인이 되었으며, 그의 시 경향은 50년대의 신비평 시론을 추구해 온 시인으로 알려져 있다. 시인은 "정말로 죽은 미국시인에게; To an American Poet Just Dead"에서 풍자적인 어조로 상업주의적 체제와 중산계급적 안일에 도취된 사회를 노래하고 이런 사회에서 시인들이 당하는 소외된 삶을 다룬다. 위의 시에서도 핵전쟁의 위협과 공포아래 존재하는 자연과 인간성의 관계를 다루고 있다.

*[제1, 2연] as you soon must(come): 조만간 오겠지만/ mad-eyed: 광기어린 눈으로/ stating the obvious: 명백한 것(사실)을 이야기하다/ not A but B: A하는 대신에 B하다(A 하지 않고 B하다)/ proclaiming our fall: 우리의 멸망을 선언하다/ their force and range: 무기들의 힘과 사정거리/ rocket the mind: 마음을 흔들다(rocket 은 여기서는 동사)/ unreckoning hearts: 셈에 능하지 못한 생각을 가진 사람들

[제3, 4연] dream of: ~에 대해 꿈꾸다/ this place without us: 우리가 없는 이 장소(이 세상)/ the leaves untroubled about us: 나무 잎들이 우리 주위에서 잠잠한 채(untroubled: 시달리지 않는, 근심 없는, 조용한)/ a stone look: 돌의 표정(모습)/ speak of: ~에 대해 이야기하시라(명령형)/ conceive: 임신하다, 마음에 품다(생각, 의견을, think나 imagine의 뜻)/ to one's cost: 손해를 입고, 쓴 맛을 보고/ crumble: 가루를 만들다, 부스러지다, crumble to dust: 부스러져 가루가 되다)/ be blackened by frost: 서리를 맞아 검게 되다/ dreamt cloud: 환상적인 구름

[5, 6연] slip into perfect shade: 완전한 그늘 속으로 사라지다(우리 시야를 떠나버리다)/ avoid the reaches of our eye: 우리의 시야를 피해버리다(시야 밖으로 사라지다)/ the jack-pine: 힘센 소나무(jack: 크고 힘이 센)/ on the cold ledge: 차디찬 벼랑 위/ lose its knuckled grip: 꽉 움켜쥔 힘을 잃고 (소나무가) 떨어져 나가다/ Xanthus: 잔터스 강/ gliding trout: 마구 뛰어놀던 송어/ dolphin's arc: 돌고래의 활선(물위로 뛰어 오름)/ 앞서의 시연과 연결되는 문장임을 유의: what should we be~?: 이 문장은 가정법의 주절로 의문문의 형태, "만일 ~들이 없다면 우리는 어떻게 될 것인가"/ without the dolphin's arc, the dove's return: 만일 돌고래의 활선과 비둘기의 귀환이 없다면, 여기서 without는 if 절을 대신함.

[7, 8, 9연] be all dispelled: 모두 없어져 버리다/ that glass obscured or broken: ~한 거울이 희미해지거나 깨질 때에(앞의 when 에 걸린다)/ the singing locust of the soul: 영혼의 노래하는 매미/ unshelled: 껍질을 벗기다(떼다)/ in which we have~와 in which beheld의 글에서 "which"는 "that glass"임/ with the worldless rose: 세계가 없는 장미(장미의 고유한 특성이 없는 장미는 아무 의미가 없다고 시인은 생각함)/ fail us: 우리를 실망시키다/ the bronze annals of the oak-tree: 참나무의 청동기(황금기를 의미함)

(역주자: 시인, 경희대 명예교수, 영문학 박사)

Appeal

I come from reading of the bygone years,
and see afar a War is being fought.
Can it be that good men are doing nought?
Can it be that they will not lend their ears?

I see Humanity has now been brought
to fight the cause of its corrupt compeers.
It is high time this dread sword disappears,
which hangs above the homes of the distraught.

'Tis time we gained mature sincerity
in spreading seeds of peace and verity,
and ending ills and madness we deplore...

Let economic structures feeding war
be turned to dust! On Earth reign evermore
the fruits of labor and prosperity!

- Translator: Helen Wohl Patterson(U.S.A)

Eno Teodoro Wanke / Brazil

- Address : Rua General Glicerio 407 ap 602 22251-Rio de Janeiro Brazil

애원

과거를 읽고 돌아와,
멀리 치열한 전쟁을 본다.
선한 사람들이 아무 일도 안할 수 있을까?
귀를 기울이지 않을 수 있겠는가?

이제 나는 타락한 동료들과 싸우기 위해
돌아오고 있는 인간애를 바라본다.
이 무서운 칼이 사라질 때이다
광인들의 집 위에 달려 있는 칼.

이제 평화와 진실의 씨를 뿌리며
성숙한 진지성을 얻을 때이다.
그리고 우리가 한탄하는 영과 광란을 마감하면서……

전쟁을 북돋우는 경제 구조는
쓰레기로 버리고! 지구상에 언제나
노동과 번영의 열매가 맺게 하자!

The Citadel of our Dreams

The citadel of our dreams
Looms behind
A Rose intertwined
With another Rose

A loving couple
In the foreground
Of our blank page

Exit from the shadows
The sculpture
Maps our future

Hédi Bouraoui/Canada

4700 Keele Street
North York
Ontario, Canada M3J 1P3

우리 꿈의 성(城)

우리 꿈의 성채는
다른 장미와 뒤엉킨
한 송이 장미 뒤에
희미하게 보인다.

우리의 비어 있는 책장 속의
정원 속에 있는
사랑의 연인들은

그림자로부터 퇴장한다.
그 조각품이
우리의 미래를 그려놓는다.

Coming Home,

The narrow lane after a long walk
A man mills around at the no name door plate
Now, the foot steps of early morning are no more found
Then, I see no shadows in between the fully grown lilac
and a pole

When a passionately burning day hides behind the violet
flower bundle
Now the dusk covers all the hopes of the world
Then, soon the insects for the night cries in loud voices
as if they no longer humiliate under the ground

Then, a man who built a temporary home
shakes his shoulder
Once he undid tightening his shirt buttons
for embracing a star
All the feet that had walked through up to this point
were getting only heavy burdens
Now again, becoming bare feet
at the dark door plate that rapped the dark moon with a cloth

- Translated into English by David S. Ro

Kim Sook-kyung(Stella)/Canada

*President of the Literary Association of the Korean Women in Canada
*Director of the Korean headquarter International Pen Club
*Director of the Seocho Literary Association, and of the Modern Poetry's Association , and of the Mungomok Literary Society
*Poetical Anthology: "Si-Wol-Ae", "A Thief of the White Paper", "Sickness for Life, Flowers, Rain"
*Prizes: Won the Best Prize of the Yun Dong-ju Literature, Won the Main Prize of the Youngrang Liteerature, and of the Prize of the Abroad Literature

귀가

먼 길 걸어온 캄캄한 골목
문패 없는 집 앞에서 서성인다
떠났던 아침의 흔적은 어디에도 없고
담 넘을 듯 자라난 라일락과 전신주 사이엔
그림자가 없다

까맣게 태운 하루는 보라의 꽃뭉치 뒤로 숨자
지상의 기다림들을 말끔히 다려놓는 땅거미
더 이상 지상의 구겨짐
낮은 곳으로 숨어들 수 없다며
저녁 풀벌레는 징하게 운다

한해살이 집 다 짓고 별을 품기 위해
와이셔츠 단추를 푼 남자
이젠 어깨를 흔든다
여기까지 걸어온 모든 발은
닳을수록 무거워지다가
달을 헝겊으로 싸맨 그믐의 문패 앞에서
다시 맨발이 되고 있다.

Prayar

Lord, Thou art in all places
forgiving the living and the dead,
always kind, Lord, Thou art like
beautiful orchards for those who are
afficted with sorrows.

Lord, Thou art in every home,
in the feverish flock, in the deserts;
Thou toucheth all harbors with Faith,
Love beneath the heavens and the seas.

Lord who grows inside of men,
Thou hast by virtue a multitude of names.
Lord of Friendship and of Hope.

It is time that Thou fulfillest the
temperance of men, the sons of Earth,
so that there may be peace, an end to war.

Lupo Hernández Rueda / Dominicana

Apartado de Correos 30323
Santo Domingo, Republica
Dominicana

기도하는 사람

신이시여, 당신은 산 자와 죽은 자를
용서하는 모든 곳에 계시며
언제나 친절하십니다.
신이시여, 당신은 슬픔으로 고통받는
사람들에겐 아름다운 정원과 같습니다.

신이시여, 당신은 모든 가정에 계시며,
열기찬 군중속에, 사막에 계십니다.
당신은 신념으로 모든 항구를 만지셨고,
사랑은 하늘과 바다 밑에 있습니다.

사람 안에서 자라시는 신이시여,
당신은 미덕에 의해 여러 이름을 가지십니다.
우정과 희망의 주인이시여.

지구의 아들이시여, 당신이
인간의 절제를 완성시키실 시간이 왔습니다.
그래서 평화와 전쟁의 끝이 깃들도록 해주소서.

Give what you like

Since I have saved your life
in the maze of the Seven Wells
you can give what you like:
a rose from the sands
a jasmine flower
the sweetness from palms
of from the leaves of mint,
the flesh of the coconut tree
or camel's milk,
or simply your smile
as bright as the sun that shines
on the cool oasis.
But,
if you have nothing to give
no flower, no fruit, no joy,
nothing at all,
I understand

Jacqueline Thévoz/England

네가 좋아하는 것을 주어라

내가 너의 생명을 구한 이래
일곱 개의 벽으로 된 미궁속에서
너는 네가 좋아하는 것을 줄 수 있다.
모래밭으로부터 한 떨기 장미를
한 송이 재스민 꽃을
종려나무나 박하잎으로부터 달콤함을
코코아나무의 신선함을
낙타의 우유를
혹은 시원한 오아시스에 비치는 태양처럼
밝고 순박한 너의 미소를
하지만,
네가 만일 아무것도 줄 것이 없다면
꽃도, 과일도, 기쁨도
전혀 아무것도 없더라도
나는 이해한다.
그리고 부탁한다. 네가 타오르는 나의 손에
한 방울의 눈물이나마 떨어뜨리길.

Old Acquaintance

I met my teenage self the other day;
She stepped out the note-books that I'd kept
And looked at me accusingly. Except
In trivialities, there was no way
I'd played the part that she had meant to play.
Hers was a mind unwilling to accept
That dreams could fail, or people prove inept,
Or good intentions suffer feet of clay.
My struggling protestations seemed uncouth.
Contrasted with the simple clarity
With whch her innocence expressed the truth.
The only sign of progress seems to be
That, whereas I admire my clear-eyed youth,
Her understanding couldn't stretch to me.

M.E.Spain/England

Flat 34 Airile House
17 Airlie Gardens LONDON
W8 7AN

오랜 사귐

나는 언젠가 나 자신의 십대(拾代) 시절을 만났다.
그녀는 내가 보관했던 공책을 들고 걷고 있었고
나를 나무라듯 보고 있었다.
사소한 것을 제외하고는
그녀가 연기하고자 했던 부분들을
내가 연기할 수 있는 방법은 없었다.
실패했던 꿈들, 또는 인간이 바보라는 것,
좋은 의도가 점토 속에 빠져 고통받는다는 사실을
받아들이고 싶지 않은 마음이었다.
나의 도전적인 항의는
진실을 표현하는 그녀의 순수하고 단순한 명백함과
비교하여 볼 때 투박한 것으로 보였다.
발전과 진보의 단 하나의 표시는
내가 맑은 눈의 젊음을 찬미하는데 비해
그녀의 이해가 나에 미칠 수 없음에 있는 듯 했다.

Embrace

I have known the brief happiness of the embrace

You have come from over the ink and the salt
My dream beyond the horizon
From over the verdant slopes of the volcanoes
Where corollas of orchids
Reach out like pink fists
And perfume the heavy dampness
You have come from beyond the Indonesian seas
Where the tepid foam of waves
Caress gently the fisherman's outrigger
From over Borneo and its blowpipes
The bamboo grown thick like leaden sheaves.

You have come from over the desert
My transcontinental love
From over the parched steppes
Where the ancient stream of Mongolian cohorts
Had ravaged the wild grass in the Siberian wind
From over the lakes with extravagant shell-fish
And the majestic descent of a certain meteor

- Translation: W.H.Goh-Chapouthier

Georges Friedenkraft/France

- Address : 11 Bis Rve du Val de Grace 75005 Paris, France

포옹

나는 포옹의 덧없는 행복을 알았다.

그대는 잉크와 소금너머로부터 왔고
수평선 너머의 내 꿈은
화산의 푸릇푸릇한 경사면 너머로부터 왔다.
난초의 꽃봉오리가
마치 분홍 손가락처럼 펼쳐지고
깊은 습지로 향기를 내뿜는 듯한 그곳으로부터
그대는 인도네시아의 바다를 건너왔나니.
따스한 포말이
어부의 돛대를 부드럽게 어루만지는 그곳
납 묶음처럼 두껍게 자란
대나무 취관(吹管)이 있는 보루네오로부터.

그대는 사막으로부터 왔나니
대륙을 건너온 내 사랑
바싹 말라붙은 걸음걸음으로
고대 몽고 보병대의 행렬이
시베리아의 바람속에서 들판을 휩쓴 곳으로부터
화려한 조개가 살고
이름모를 유성의 웅대한 추락이 있는 호수로부터,

Horses

Symmetry of motion,
unattainably tender
looseness of limbs,
classic stretching of bodies,
of rearing tails,
spontaneous pas de quatre of hoofs,
fleeing manes in the flying wind:
individuality used to flights;
skill to survive since millenniums,
original harmony in perfection,
culmination of a creation
which melt away us in our hands.

Hans Dieter Lücke/Germany

Winklertr. 4 a
1000 Berlin 33
Tel. 030/891 57 83

말[馬]

동작의 균정(均整)
무한이 부드럽고
시원스러운 사지(四肢),
고전적으로 쭉 뻗은 동체(胴體),
위로 솟구친 꼬리,
자동적으로 움직이는 네 개의 발굽들,
휫날리는 바람결에 도망치는 갈기털:
도망치는 개성(個性)
수천 년 전부터 오래오래 살아 남은 비결,
완성 속에
이미 예정된 조화
우리의 두 손 밑에서 녹아 버리는
어떤 창조의 정점(頂点).

Shantytown, Cape of Good Hope

A place where men just wait,
and hope is in the waiting:
vivid with the stains of life,
open to the moon's clean wash,
the feel of the rain just failling,
the sound and smell of sea-
where pinched, deprived old faces
show a beauty in repose.

H.F.Noyes/Greece

C/O MNK PRODUCTIONS
10, DIMOKRITOU
KOLONAKI
ATHENS, GREECE 10673

빈민굴, 희망봉

인간이 기다리는 곳.
그리고 희망은 기다림 속에 있다.
인생의 오점으로 생생한
달의 깨끗한 여울로 열려진
빗방울이 떨어지는 느낌
바닷소리와 바닷내음－
옛 얼굴들을 괴롭히고 빼앗은
휴양중인 한 美人을 보여준다.

President--(God)

President: Oh my President,
My meditation is to love the Labour Lady
Her skin is tost like midnight sky,
Neither she has cloth nor purse
But she is nymph!

I vaunt for my love
She is vegeted by Laborious jin
What a melodious Tune and witty,
Merely I love for melody.

Nether she has hut nor a loft
She is joyous for her ivy garden
Is my crime for my love?

President! Oh my President
My lover is laborious
No need obdurute, or to push gloom
She is pure and beauty like nymph.

Bidhan Datta / India

10 Deshbandhu Road(East)
Calcutta-700 035
India

I love the Labour Lady--
Please come I and you pursuance
For ever like a speedy shorting star
The work is worship
Your indulgent love is invitable work
You love her
I love the labour lady
By your bless

통치자시여(신이시여)

통치자시여, 오 나의 통치자시여,
저의 심사숙고는 노동의 여인을 사랑하는 것입니다
그녀의 피부는 밤하늘처럼 시달려 있습니다
그녀는 옷도 지갑도 없습니다
그러나 그녀는 요정입니다

나는 나의 사랑을 자랑합니다
그녀는 저의 노동복 청바지로 푸르러집니다
곡조 있는 노래와 위트,
나는 단지 곡조를 사랑합니다

그녀는 오두막도 다락방도 없고
그녀는 그녀의 상아빛 전원에서 기뻐합니다
나의 사랑이 과연 죄가 됩니까?

통치자시여, 나의 통치자시여,
저의 애인은 부지런히 일을 합니다
아무 완고함도 필요없고 어둠을 밀어냅니다
그녀는 요정처럼 순수하고 아름답습니다
나는 그 노동의 여인을 사랑합니다
부디 오셔서 나와 당신이 빠른 유성처럼
영원히 노동을 추구하도록 해 주소서

Translation

I do not say how the flower
come by the tree dead;
nor where the desperation flowers
between ters and looks;
but neither I know where the flowers,
without noise, colours the petals
for the butterfly falling in love;
unfortunately I do not know nor
how under the snow lies the silence of desires;
neither where the freezed flower of the lake
goes when the sun dissolve it;
but I know exatly when
the eyes-wonder become flowers
of love, when the springtime
builds the games for the bees,
the swallow, the children
in to the gardens.
The heart of the world.

Adalia Negri Lavagnoli / Italia

- Address : Born Cremona 15.10.1936 Residence: Via Pietro Agosti, 59 (18038) Sanremo(IM) Italia

해석

나는 죽은 나무 곁에
어떻게 꽃이 피는 지를 말하지 않는다;
절망이 눈물과 모습 사이
어느 곳에서 피어나는 지도;
나는 알지 못한다.
꽃이 사랑에 빠진 나비를 위해
소리없이 꽃잎을 물들이는 곳을;
불행하게 나는 모른다.
어떻게 눈 아래에 말없는 욕망이 놓여 있는지를;
해가 호수의 빙화를 녹을 때
빙화가 어디로 사라지는 지도 모른다.
그러나
나는 분명히 안다.
언제 경의의 눈이 사랑의 꽃으로 되는 때를
봄날이 정원에 꿀벌, 제비, 어린이를 위한
유희를 만드는 때를.
미움의 세계를

The Adriatic

The brooms on golden slops
liht over the shores
with a sad greeting
towards the dying sea;
mucilages run adrift.
The lands of precious memories
are the blue sea's widows
to whom the throb of the shiny history
was committed on the wave's throb.
Wuill the earth and the sea of our fathers
be able to get married again
despite any pollutioun?
Meanwhile the sea gull is fluttering on the wave
the shell is rolling upon the beach
and they seehm to be waiting...

Rosa Sabbieti / Italia

- Address : 62100 Macerata, Corso Cavour 50, Italia

아드리아 해

황금 사면(斜面) 위의 금작화는
사멸해 가는 바다를 향해
슬픈 인사를 하며
해안가를 부유한다;
바다 생물들이 쏟아낸 점액이 수면 위를 타다니고
소중한 기억의 대지는
반짝이는 역사의 고동을
일렁이는 파도에 내맡긴 이들에게
푸른 바다의 창들이 된다
우리 조상들의 땅과 바다가
오염에도 불구하고
다시 결합할 수 있을까?
갈매기는 파도 위에서 날아다니고
조개들은 해안가에 널려
무언가를 기다리는데……

White Porcelain

Gazing at the flawless
White porcelain

Reflected by a sorrowful heart,
Porcelain
Shines palely and
Is disappearing
Far in the distance.

O, Pale soul
Melting into
The prayer--

Jun Ueno/Japan

- Born in Osaka, Japan in 1963.
- Graduated Doshisha university faculty of literature(majored in aesthetics and art philosophy).
- Studied the poetry of Yun Dong-Ju in Seoul, Korea from 1992 to 1995 and received strong influence from him.
- Married in Seoul. Wife is Korean.
- A member of Japan Poets Club.
- A member of the Japanese poetry magazine "Saku"
- Writing poems and essays for introducing Japanese poets into Korea in the Korean poetry magazine "Munye Han-Kuk"
- Visiting professor in Sunchon national university branch of Japanese language and literature.

(Works)
'The footprints in a desert'(poems)
'Heaven, Wind, Stars and Poetry'(Japanese translation of Yun Dong-Ju's poems)
'A poet who sings stars - poems and studies of Yun Dong-Ju'(Collaborating)

백자(白磁)

흠 하나 없는
백자(白磁)를 쳐다본다.

슬픈 마음에 비춰져
자기(磁器)는
창백한 빛을 내며
아득한 곳으로
사라져 간다.

아아, 기도 속으로
스며드는
창백한 혼(魂)이여—

白磁

疵一つ無い
白磁の器に見入る

哀しみの心に映えて
器は
蒼ぎめた光彩(ひかり)を放ち
幽遠の彼方に
沈んでいく

ああ, 祈りのなかに
溶けていく
蒼白な魂よ―

Jangbaek Falls

The wavering flowers around a Jangbaek fall
That the wild flowers with many colores
Are boomed splendidly,

A patriotic soul, remained image as a boy
Named Kim Byeong-(cheon)su in Yeoju, an army of national independence
Who made his way through the vast Manchurian fields.

The water-apricot named 'Suchuri'
Is the waving dance
The flower stalks blooming again
As fragrance of the yellow iris flower,

Ah,
The spray of water, a patriotic spirit of the Jangbaek Falls!

- Tr. by Won Eung-Soon

*[Note] A famous army of national independence named Kim Gu as an acting chairman in the temporary government, sought for Kim Byeong-(cheon)su's house of his birth and remained a "Wielding Brush".

Ahn Geum-shik/Korea

*The first debut as a Poet from the Hanmak(monthly magazine)
*Service as a Member of Advisory Committee at Kyounggi-do
*Service as an Officer of the Public Information of National Policy
*Director, the Society of the World Poetry
*A Planning Committee of U-Ang Group*Service as a Director of Yeoju Culture Organization
*(Present) Head Vice-president of the General Allies for a Righteous Army Memorial works

장백폭포

오방색 야생화
흐드러지게 핀
장백폭포 언저리 꽃너울

광활한 만주벌판 누빈
애국혼 여주 소년 독립군
17살 나이 김병(천)수의 잔영

수추리 물매화
샛노란 붓꽃 향으로
다시 피는 꽃 대궁의
너울춤

아아
장백폭포 애국 혼
물보라여!

* 김구 수반이 귀국하여 김병(천)수 여주 소년 독립군 생가 방문하여 휘호 남김

Living(Life)

Getting to the place
We cannot dream more,

Getting to the place
We cannot return to
Our birth's time more,

Half a day of the season
Is dozing.

O, this wave
Is surprising.

- Tr. by Won Eung-Soon

Ahn Yong-suk/ Korea

*Member of the Korean Poets' Association
*Member of the Korea headquarter, in the International Pen Club
*Member of the Literary Society of the World Poetry
*E-Mail: ahhn@hanmail.net
*Address: Angok-Ro4, Samik Apt. 208-705, Bucheon City, Kyeonggi-Do, Korea

삶

더는, 꿈꿀 수 없는 곳에
이르러,

더는
생시로 돌아갈 수 없는 곳에
이르러,

한 시절의 한나절이
졸고 있네

오, 놀라운
이 물결.

I Didn't Have the Heart to Pick the Moon

The moonlight was so beautiful,
I wanted to pick the moon and to see it in the room,
But I didn' t have the heart to pick it
Lest its beautiful light should be lost.

The starlight was so beautiful,
I wanted to pick the star and to see it in the room,
But I didn' t have the heart to pick it
Lest its pretty light should be deprived of in the room.

Your light was so lovely(fair),
I wanted to pick it and to see it in my heart,
But I didn' t have the heart to pick it and to see,
For fear of losing your light in my bosom.

Ah, Longing Lover,
Ah, Sweet Lover!
I would rather be better to lose my light
In order to display your light freely.

- Tr. by Won Eung-Soon

Bae Byeong-gun/ Korea

*Member of "the General Arts and Culture of Yu-Sugn"
*Member of the Songwriter's Association of Korea
*Selected as a Good Essay in an Essay Part of "the Teacher's Literature" in Seoul(2018)
*First Debut as a new Poet from "the General Arts and Culture of Yu-Sung"(2019)/ and as a new Essayist from "the General Arts and Culture of Yu-Sung"(2019)
*Address: (Zip Code 08855) #73-14 Nangog-ro 26 gil, Samwon Hights Ville, No. 401, Kwanak-gu, Seoul City, Korea
*Phone Number: 010-5408-6348

차마 따지 못했습니다

달빛이 너무나 아름다워
달을 따다 방에 놓고 싶지만
방에서는 그 아름다운 빛을 잃을까 하여
차마 따지 못했습니다.

별빛이 너무나 예뻐서
별을 따다 방에 놓고 싶지만
방에서는 그 예쁜 빛을 잃을까 하여
차마 따지 못했습니다.

그대 빛이 너무나 고와서
그대를 따다 제 맘에 놓고 싶지만
제 맘에서는 그 고운 빛을 잃을까 하여
차마 따지 못했습니다.

아 그리운 그대여
아 고운 그대여
그대가 그대 빛을 자유로이 발하도록
차라리 저의 빛을 잃으렵니다.

The Wine Named Tears

The two eyes facing to face with a cup of wine,
Are filled with its water color.

The sadness already
Flowed over the banks of heart,
Whether I drink wine,
Or scoop out.

I didn't say to the last
A word of consolation
That I would say directly
And only chewing up like gum,

Bae Young-suk/ Korea

*Born ar Suncheon, Jeonnam, Korea
*President of "the Suncheon Association of Literature", and of "the Gangnam Literary Society"
*Poetical Anthology: <The Poor Seoul>, <Yearning on the Curtain of White Cloth>, <For the Aching Name>
*Prizes: Won the Prize of the Suncheon Art,
Won the Prize of the Suncheon Writer of Literature
*(present) *Adviser of the Suncheon Literary Association
*Director of the Literary Association of Jeonnam
*Teacher of Seungpyung Middle School
*Address: (Zip Code 58015) #96 Sindae-ro, 306dong 705(Jungheung S-Class) Haeryong-myeon, Suncheon City, Jeonnam, Korea

'After getting out debt,
I was 40 years old over,
The young dream vanished
Like a funeral ode'

I drank the wine named tears
As much as getting drunk
Because his heart like bloody water
Had seen before me fairly.

- Tr. by Won Eung-Soon

눈물 술

술잔을 마주한 두 눈에
물빛이 가득 찼다

술을 마시는 건지
눈물을 퍼내는 건지
이미 슬픔은
마음 둑을 범람해 있었다

빗 고개를 넘고 나니
어느새 지천명을 지났고
푸른 꿈이 만장처럼
사라졌다는 그

입술을 맴도는
위로의 말 끝끝내 하지 못하고
애먼 것들만
질겅질겅 씹는데

핏물 같은 그의 심장이
선연히 보여
취하도록
눈물 술을 마시고 말았다.

Dalgaebi and Boraegi

Boraegi tells a Dalgaebi's life,
Looking at me openly,
"My name is so good
That I was welcome by the beautiful lady."

But I(Dalgaebi) am not concerned with the name,
Only trying to bloom the flower.
And keeping its own toughness in its life,
In its breeding of race is different from others.

If trying to tear it to kill,
It's good to increase its numbers.
So if putting in the fire, it's as good as in the flowers,
Floating on water, it's as fresh as bathing,
And if putting on the wall,

Bang Jung-sun/Korea

*Awarded new-poet prize from monthly "Literature and Arts" in 2001.
*Director, the Society of the World Poetry
*Member of the World Poetry Research Institute.
*Won the Main Prize of the World Poetry"
*Address: 360, jaryong-ri, Sangha-myeon, Gochang-gun, Jeonbuk, Korea
*Tel : 010-6770-0481

It's as interesting as getting on a swing and singing a song,
So increasing numbers its own race,
I(Dalgaebi) furnish man with a medical use.
Boraegi with a good name, and only a telltale doing harm,
What have you done.

- Tr. by Won Eung-Soon

달개비와 보래기

달개비의 삶을 말한다
보래기는 나를 보며 하는 말이
자기는 이름이 좋아 아가씨의
대접을 받는다고 입 성근 소리를 한다

하지만 나는 꽃을 피워 내며
그 이름 관계하지 않는다
일생에 강인함을 간직하며
종족에 번식 또한 남다르다

아무리 죽이려고 찢어놓으면
형제가 많아서 좋고
불속에 넣으면 꽃 속에 있어 좋고
물에 띄우면 시원한 목욕재계 정말 좋아
담장에 얹어 놓으면 그넷줄 흔들흔들
노래하며 놀고
그리하여 나는 종족을 널리 퍼지게 하며
사람에게 약용으로 제공도 한다
이름 좋은 보래기는 무엇을 하였는가
해로움만 끼쳐 주는 말만 좋은 보래기는!

At the Great Wall of China

Standing on the first stone staircase of the Great Wall of China,

What should make them
Pile up the Great Wall?

It would be only for his glory and honor
Rather than for his people.

Only the yearning of a millenium
Are coming down on the stone staircase to soak,

Getting to its summit,
Eternity seems to be a dream(ksana).

Cho Keum-ja / Korea

* Pen names: Eunsung
* Graduated from the Graduate of Administration in Wonkwang Univ.
* Started literary career through "literary movement & Trend" in 2005.
* Received the first prize at a prize contest for woman essay writer that seohai broad casting superintend.
* President of jeonbuk woman's tennis club
* Member of the society of world poetry research institute
* Won a commendation of President
* Won a Prize for Filial Conduct

Won a Prize of 40 Years Service at the Red Cross Society (Jean-Henri Dunant' s Prize).

* Chairman of Industrial Construction at Gochang County Assembly.
* Publication : "A Treasure Put in a Pottery"(2013)

* Address: 40-8, Seongsan 4gil, Gochang-eup, Gochang-gun, Jeon-buk, Korea.
* Tel : 010-6228-2211

Being exposed to the cold wind with foggy rains,
Indulging in my own notion,

Si-Emperor of Jin-nation of China coveting gain and long life,
Has gone nowhere to be seen,

A medicine for immortality in his nation
Is of no use for his death.

Being exposed to a nasty rain,
My steps also are heavy.

- Tr. by Won Eung-Soon

만리장성에서

만리장성 첫 돌단에 서서

그 무엇이 밀려와서
만리장성을 쌓아야 했을까!

백성을 위하기보다
끊을 수 없는 영욕이리.

천년의 그리움만 돌 더미에
내려앉아 스며드는데

정상에 올라서니
영겁이 꿈만 같네.

안개비에 차가운 바람 맞으며
상념에 잠기는데

부귀영화 누리려던 진시황은
간 데 없고

도성 안에 불사약도
죽는 데는 허사로고!

궂은비 맞으며
발걸음도 무겁구나.

Before the Judge

At the beginning of one spring, I needs a clothes to cover my naked body From long, long ago;
It's because, in summer, a fig tree of wide leaves in Eden can conceal Myself. And, from now on, thinking of not being uncovered by anybody,
I hid all that I had belonged to. But, in autumn, what I had in mind are,
I feel, getting nerves for fear of one or two being found.
People gathered together in twos and threes in the plaza.
Before them at last came the Last day of the Judgement.
There were

Cho Son-hyong / Korea

*Born at Pocheon, Geonggi-Do, Korea
*First Debut as a Poet from the Monthly "the Munhaksege(Literary World)" With a Prize of a new Poet(1993)
*Literary Works: "At the Lake the Train Stopped too", "A sluice", "The Waterway(Anthology in English)",
* Prose Collection: "Morning of a Zelkova Tree"
*Member of the Korean Writers' Association, *Adviser of "Literature and Arts of City" and of "the Ivy Literature", *President of Tancheon Literary Association (in Sungnam City)", *(The former) Lecturer of the English language and Literature at Daejin Univ. *Ph. Degree of English Literature.
*Awarding: 1) The Order of Okjokeunjeong (August, 2010)
2) The 24th the Main Literary Gold Prize of Heonanseolheon
*Address: (Post No: 13517) #124 Yatap-Ro, Topmaeul 605-1001, Bundang-Gu, Seongnam City, Geonggi-Do, Korea
*E-mail: sunhjo@hanmail.net

Wind,
Sunbeam,
And water was there:
But, as they could not be the real judge, I had no choice but to wait.
On a rainy day of autumn leaves, I came out to the plaza
And couldn't help surrendering.
" O Lord, I'm naked! in the end"

Winter is like a mirror.
I stand in front of Him in a shameful look.

심판자 앞에서

따스한 봄기운이 일던 그 날로부터 앙상한 내 나신(裸身)에 걸칠 것을 찾습니다. 오래도록 기다렸습니다. 여름이 오면 에덴동산의 무화과 같은 넓적하고 커다란 잎으로 몸에 감출 수 있으니까요. 이제부턴 아무에게도 영영 발각되지 않을 거라는 생각으로 희희낙락 열심히 감추었습니다. 가을이 되어 내 안에 것들이 서서히 불안해합니다. 감춘 것이 하나둘 드러날까 봐서 말입니다.

광장엔 삼삼오오 사람들이 몰려옵니다. 심판이 왔기 때문입니다.
바람,
햇볕,
물이 있었지만 진정한 심판자는 아니었습니다. 그것은
기다림뿐이었습니다.
늦가을 비오는 날 나는 거리로 나와 항복할 수밖에 없었습니다.
"오, 주여! 난, 끝내 발가벗고 말았습니다!"

겨울은 거울과 같은 존재입니다.
나는 부끄러운 모습으로 그 앞 서 있습니다.

A Soliloquy of Water

Water always wishes to flow
As an original mind,
And to be a clear and cool song of its gesture,
A clear and cool song,
Even it is flowing,
That dirty things are not inserted
However it has
Broad shoulders,

Today, only shuddering
At nauseating things,
It feels so hard as to be sick

Choi Seung-beom / Korea

* Born in Namwon. A poet. A doctor of literature
* A professor emeritus of Cheonbuk Univ.
* A superintendent at Goha Literature attached to Cheonju star bank
* Started a literary career(Korean poem) through Heondai(modern) literature in 1958
* A manager of Cheonju branch office of Korea Writer Association
* Awarded Jeongwun Sijo(Korean poem) literary, Korea Modern poem literary, Garam sijo literary, Korea Literary, Mokjeong Literary, Nation Literary, Korean Poem Literary(in the first bout of its ceremony)
*Advisor, the Society of the World Poetry
* A literary work : Study on Korean Essay, The Fragrance of Namwon, Virtue and Vice are All My Teacher, Essay about Korean Poem, Flower-A Woman-Times, A Sound etc.
* Poetical works : In front of an Orchid, Nature's Monologue, A Journey to Mongolia, At the Crater Lake on Mt. Paekt, Hiding Myself with a Withered Leaf etc.

As to breathe one clear respiration out,
Finally
Is its own original mind going to be rot?
Or is it a poison?

How can we moisten our throats?

- Tr. by Won Eung-Soon

물의 독백

본디 마음으로
하냥 흐르고 싶다
가슴 넓다 해도
더러운 것 끼지 않는
청렬한
흘러도 청렬한 몸짓
노래이고
싶다

오늘도 구역질에
몸서리 칠 뿐
맑은 숨 한 번 내쉬재도
지쳐 병 들고
끝내는
저 본디 마음
썩어나는가
독인가

어이 목을 축이겠는가

A Weaving Woman Living in Solitude

The snowy night at the coldest winter month,
Why was the night at that time so long?

The sound weaving a lonesome atmosphere
In one stitch after one stitch with snapping, snapping,

The haggard face shone in a flickering lamplight
Whom I stole a look at,
Was a woman full of grief.

I knew not
Such inner concealed state
Of a weaving woman living in solitude
As the fox in a back hill set off pining for her lover,
But how could he smelled out the inner fact delicately

Choi Sun-ae / Korea

*Debuted as poet by Han maek Literature
*Pubisher. Member of Korea Literature Association, The World Poetry Research, Suncheon Literature club, leader of Pilmar Literaler club.
*Director, the Society of the World Poetry
*Collection of Poems:
"The Way to the Home Town"
"One Sided Love of the Flower Buds"
"The Poet' s Trumpet"

*Address : 489-1 Jekok-dong Suncheon-City Jeonnam Korea

And only thinking of the red-ripe persimmon
In the round reed-made basket on the shelf?

Taking off a piece of reeding, the loom's tool
She wore from her waist, and the heel she put on,
You, giving him the red-persimmon on the shelf silently,
And when soothing her crunchy mind with only one radish,
The night when the white snow falls down,
Why would I pine for the night at that time so?

- Tr. by Won Eung-Soon

독수공방 베 짜는 여인

동지섣달 하얀 눈 내리던 밤
그때 그 밤은 왜 그리도 길었을까

고요한 적막(寂寞)을 한 땀 한 땀 짜올리는 소리
찰가닥 찰가닥

살며시 눈 떠보면
가물거린 등잔불에 비친 야윈 얼굴
설움 가득 고인 여인

뒷산 여우
님 그리워 울어가는지
독수공방 베 짜는 여인의
속내 난 알 바 없고
선반 위 놓인 둥근 대바구니
감홍시 생각만 뽀시락뽀시락
그 속내 어찌 알아챘을까

허리에 찬 바디 풀어 벗고
발꿈치에 신은 끄시기도 벗고
살며시 선반 위 내주던 감홍시
당신은 무 하나 아삭아삭 타는 속내 달래는
그때 그 하얀 눈 내리던 밤
그때 그 밤은 왜 그리도 그리울까

A Way for my Hometown

A way for my hometown
Is already awake even at midnight.
The floating clouds and mountains in my childhood
And my hometown on the way is also awake as yet.
The rural way going for my hometown
Is making civilization go ahead.
The blurred shape of a totem
Which I come across at the rural way
Going for my hometown,
Your naivety enduring through long years!
Gazes at tomorrow
With overflowing custom.
The rustic way going for my home town
May be an outing of each one for a spring garden.

- Tr. by Won Eung-Soon

Chong Song-jon / Korea

*Graduated from Dept. of Jungang Univ. & the Graduate School of Jungang Univ..
*Retired as a Principal of Jukjeon Middle School, Yongin, Geonggido.
*Recommended as a poet from the magazine, "Poetry and Poetics", 1962.
*Taught as a Inviting Professor of Keonggi Univ.
*Representative Prof. of 'Gwangju Literary Art Collete'.
*Served as a Chairman of 'the Gwangju Forum', Geonggido.
* Served as a President of the World Poetry.
*A Member of the Literary Men's Association of Korea.
*A Central Committee of the Modern Literary Association.
*Won the 'Great' Prize from "the Literary Movement & Trend ", (1998).
*Won the 'Original' Prize from the Freedom Poets Association, (2000).
*Poetic Anthology: <The Weight of Longing>, <The Silence of Wind>, etc.

고향 길

고향으로 가는 길은
한밤중에도 이미 깨어 있다
둥둥 떠 있는 어릴 적 구름과 산
그 길에 아직도 고향은 깨어 있다
고향으로 가는 시골 길은
문명을 앞서가고 있다
고향으로 가는 시골 길에서
만나는 장승의
흐릿한 형상은
긴 세월을 살아온 소박함이여
넘쳐흐르는 풍습으로
내일을 바라본다
고향으로 가는 시골 길은
저마다 봄동산 나들이다.

The Rose-colored Sunset

If the heaven falls in love,
How could it help its inner burning mind?

Whether it's accidental or inevitable,
In the last moment finishing its life
With such rose-colored breast and as coughing up blood,
Burning up in flame with all its passion!

In fact, doing all the best is the beautiful art,
And makes even all natural things
So solemn as entranced,

They are secret result of providence of God, for 12 months a year,
And are joy, anger, sorrow and pleasure of fragrant human life,

---

Chun Byung-ok/Korea

*Cheon Byeong-ok
*First Debut as a new Poet from the Global Literature(2005).
*Member of the Korea Writers' Association og Korea, of the Global Writers' Meeting, of the Korea Race Literature, of the Yesarang Female Literature, and of the World Poetry.
*Vice President of the Korea Race Literature.
*Poetical Anthology: <The Rose-colored Sunset>
*Address: #20 Jeonja-ro 123gil, Edenheights no. 302, Jangan-gu, Suwon city, Geongi-do, Korea.
*Email: chun9459@hanmail.net
*HP : 010-4893-7701

Today I, giving a big applause at his providence,
And fascinating a west heaven
By beauty of humanness in a single time,

I want to raise that rose-colored sunset
Solemnly in my life
Which has sublimed even pains with beauty.

- Tr. by Won Eung-Soon

장밋빛 노을

하늘도 사랑을 하면
타는 속마음을 어쩔 수 없는가

우연이든 필연이든
끝을 다하는 마지막 삶의 순간에
각혈하듯 저리도 붉은 장밋빛 가슴으로
뜨겁게 열정을 다해 불타오름이여

정녕 최선은 아름다운 예술
자연만물까지도 황홀히
숙연하게 하나니

일년 열두달 신의 비밀의 손길
향기로운 인생의 희로애락

나는 오늘도 유정의 미로
서녘하늘을 단번에 사로잡는
위대한 섭리에 큰 갈채를 보내면서

아픔마저 아름다움으로
승화시키는 저 장밋빛 노을을
내 생애에 엄숙히 올리고 싶다

The Chestnut's Fragrance

Burying a grain of chestnut under the stove,
Smelling a June's scent around its ashes,
Bees and butterflies brought its scent all,
Only to be remained is a baldhead in the empty shell(skin).

Burying memories of the sweet sixteen youth,
Raising ashes in his way to arrive not very long,
Together with a strip's sound crying in Ba-re-re Ha-re-re.
Oh, Quit! the chestnut's flowers pop out with a sound of Tok-Tok.

- Tr. by Won Eung-Soon

Chung Jee-hong / Korea

*Born at Kyungnam, in 1958
*Graduated at Kyung Hee Univ.
*Member of the Writers' Association of Korea
*Member of the Writers of the Thought and Literature
& it's a Steering Committee
*An Inspector, the Society of the World Poetry
*Chairman of the Literary Society of the 'Goeungeul'
*Present: Trading Business & Agriculture
*Rubits Apt. 101-305, Shinpungdong, Gimje City, Jeonbuk, Korea
*Tel: 010-9340-2321

밤꽃 향기

화덕불 뒤적거려 밤톨을 묻고
재를 다독여 유월 향기 맡자니
향기야 모두 벌 나비 가져가고
갑골 껍질에 민 대머리 남았네

만화방창 이팔청춘 기억을 묻어
여삼추 남은 길에 재를 돋우니
바르르 하르르 문풍지 우는 소리
아서라 톡톡 밤꽃 밤꽃 터지네

A Full Moon

The Moon with being delivered of a baby and going back, reached a bamboo grove.
The tough and ruthless things got the worst of it here all,
The bamboo-leaves like the seaweed bated their breath,
She didn't straightened herself, so one buttock floated up in the air.

As the round love waxes again from the place the wisdom tooth cut,
The round things hold more than they might expect as one,
The hoarsened voice throws into confusion.

The bamboo bush, sweeping over as blooming bean and scallion, dawn!
That silence, that thunderbolt, that extravagant buttocks,
Who could lend a hand with it?

- Tr. by Won Eung-Soon

Gwon O-un/ Korea

* First Debut as a New Poet from the Shinchun-Munye of Chosun Daily Newspaper(1966)
* Literary Action: Member of Literary Coterie, "The Shinchun Poetry", "The Poetics"
* Editorial Journalist of Student's Magazine, "Hak-Won"(1968)
* Editorial Director of the Female Encyclopedia, KBS(1966)
* Professor at Dept. of Literary Arts and Creative Writing, Jungang Univ. as Holding Double Jobs
* Literary Works: "Correcting the Korean Language", "The Korean Language Spoiled by Writers", "1234 Miss-Using Words of the High brows", "A Great Dictionary for Spacing Words", "The Korean Language the Poets Spoiled"

보름

몸 풀고 돌아가던 달이 대숲에 들었습니다
여기서는 질기고도 모진 것들 다 혼이 빠졌는지
미역귀 같은 댓잎들이 숨을 죽이는데
미처 여미지 못해서 엉덩이도 하나 둥두렷이 솟았습니다

사랑니 빠진 자리에서 다시 둥근 사랑 차오르듯
둥근 것들은 하나같이 속에 궁글어
잠긴 목소리도 우렁우렁 속이 뒤집힙니다

노굿 일듯 휩쓸고 나온 대숲이여, 새벽이여
저 고요, 저 벼락, 저 엉뚱한 엉덩이
누가 손 좀 볼 수 있겠습니까?

The Scripture as a Whistle

At the eulalia field of the Sky Garden, they say,
The silver-haired uncle who descended from a westerner's blood,
Is opening a large book to read for us,

And a width of sound, being heard fluttering in the wind,
The more going near to him, the more it is moved,
They say,'to scatter is to die' 'so sit head to head',
'Bend our body as the wind blow',
The book is written by bury(conceal) his feet into the inner part of the universe,

---

Han Jung-won/ Korea

*Born in Seoul
*First Debut as a new Poet from a Quarterly Magazine, 'Munyesajo' (1998)
*Graduated from Dept. of Creative Works, the Art Graduate School of Jungang Univ.
*General Director of Seocho Literary Association
*Vice President of the Jipshin Literary Society
*Member of the Korean Writers' Association
*Director of the School of Education for Statement named Readers, Apgujeong
*Awarding Prizes: Won the Prize of the Jipshin Literature
Won the Main Prize of the Munyesajo(the Trend of Literature)
*Literary Works: "Reading & Writing A Juvenile Story for Fostering the Power of Imagination and Creation(Joint Work)"
'The Creative Statement for Reading as a Juvenile Story(60 vols)
*Poetical Anthology: "A Cup of Coffee, Taking off Clothes"
* E-mail : leaders7@hanmail.net

The book's leaves are too big for anyone to turn over them,
Though the north wind blows and the snow falls in the cold winter,
Saying a word of the King Solomon again,
'These would be passed',
This grand scripture, caused to ferment tears
Was become now that we could hear only as a whistle.

- Tr. by Won Eung-Soon

휘파람 경전

하늘공원 억새밭에는
서양인의 피를 받은 은빛머리 아저씨가
커다란 책을 펼쳐 들고 책을 읽어 준다지

가까이 가면 갈수록 바람에 펄럭이며 들려오는
소리의 광폭이 더욱 감동적이라는데
흩어지면 죽는다며 어깨를 맞대고
바람이 불면 부는 대로 휘어지며
우주 속살에 발을 묻으며 만든 책장이란다

책장은 하도 커서 누구도 넘길 수가 없다지
추운 겨울 삭풍이 몰려오고 눈비가 내려도
'이것 또한 지나가리라'
솔로몬 왕자의 말씀을 되뇌이며
울음을 삭힌 커다란 책은
이제 휘파람 소리로만 들을 수 있는
경전이 되었다지.

If Autumn Comes, I Would Go Home.

Autumn is far advanced, it calls winter.
Winter shall come as autumn has been far advanced in my hometown?
Autumn leaves with all red colors climb up high to the sky.
Does a wind of late autumn blow to my home town?
Though spring, summer, autumn, and winter
As a migratory bird, in the deep autumn night
That I am full of troubles,
Friend! your face stays in your eyes,
Singing a song of home along with stars,
If autumn comes, I would go to hometown on clouds.

Hong Chun-pyo/Korea

*Pen name: Cheong-myeong
*Born in 1943 Imsil, Jeonbuk, Korea
*Graduated from Graduate school, Ph.D.(Political Science)
*Made a new Debut as a Poet(2003) from the Literary Essay(Public Official's Lit. Quarterly Magazine)
*Chairman of Guro Writers' Association
*Director of the Korea Writers' Association
*Member of International PEN
*Director oof the Korea Public Official's Association
*The 5th Chairman of Guro Ward Assemblyman
*Publication: *I Want to Live as a Pine tree, its Vine(1st Poetic Anthology), People in Oppositive Way(2nd Poetic Anthology), A Postbox that is not Solitary, Happiness of Satisfaction in the Real Life
*Receiving Prize
*Won the Order of President(National Service Merit)
*Won the Writer's Prize of the Good Literature
*Won the 14th Main Prize of the Korea Race Literature
*Address: 136-40 Guro 6dong, Nayang BLD, no. 101, Guro-gu, Seoul, Korea

Autumn is far advanced, it calls me to my hometown.
Does the inner mind of mine go to my hometown?
I also would go to heaven as an autumn leave.
Has autumn of my home been far advanced?
As the arrogant golden waves of Sumjin River,
In this autumn night that my mind is hanging around,
Friend! your voice goes past by ears,
Singing a song of homesickness with that full moon,
If autumn comes, I would go to my hometown on the wind.

- Tr. by Won Eung-Soon

가을이 오면 고향 가네

가을은 깊어 겨울 부르네
고향에 가을 깊어 겨울 오는가?
만색홍엽이 창공 오르네
고향에 늦가을 바람 부는가?
봄, 여름, 가을, 겨울 철새 따라
내 마음 시름하는 가을밤에
친구야! 네 얼굴이 눈가에 앉아
저 별들과 애향가 부르며
가을이 오면 구름 타고 고향 가네

가을은 깊어 향수 부르네
고향에 내 마음 가고 있는가?
나도 낙엽 되어 하늘 가네
고향에 늦가을은 깊어 가는가?
섬진강 도도한 금물결 따라
내 마음 서성이는 가을밤에
친구야! 네 음성이 귓전에 스쳐
저 보름달과 망향가 부르며
가을이 오면 바람 타고 고향 가네

Peeling the Garlics

The fat sinew lost its weight(grew thin),
The garlics which are picked up from a jar spent last year,
And they aren't old, but their face are haggard
And their sinews grew thin.
They pulled light body in and are hugged in plain water
They are put(filled) into water with light body themselves.
The garlics that filled their body with water
Are floating lightly carelessly to make irrelevant remarks.
The good quality of garlic has nutritive value,

Hong Yun-pyeo/Korea

*Poet, Juvenile Writer, Honorary Ph.D. of Literature
*Born at Dangjin, Chungnam, Korea
*Kyung Hee Univ., Graduate School of Public Administration(M. A. Degree)
*First Debut as a new Poet through 'the Literary World' and 'the Sijo Literature'
*Poetical Anthology: "Overcoming the Winter Season": "A Village of Cranes": "Dreaming Grand Bridge of West Sea"; "A Great Outing"; and "A Danjin Poet", "A Red Rainbow" etc.
*The Sijo Anthology: "Mt. Amis Azaleas!"; " The Mother's Night", etc.
*Awarding Prizes: Won the great Prize of the Chungnam Literature; the Prize of the Okro-Literature; the Prize of the Heo-kyun Literature; the Prize of the Korea Farmer's Literature; the Prize of the Literature and Arts of the Korea and Chinese; the Prize of the Hwang-hee Literature; and the Prize of the Present Time(the Dangjin Foundation), etc.
*A Committee of the Korea Writers' Association; A Director of the Korea PEN, in International PEN; of the Korea Poet's Association; of the Society of the World Poetry, etc.
*(Present) Vice President of the Chungnam Writers' Association, President of the Dang-jin Writers' Association, Adviser of the Society of the Hosu Poetry. etc.
*Address: (Nuskin Dangjin Center) 238-1, Eupnae-dong, Dangjin City, Chungnam, Korea.
*Tel: 041-355-3844 Mobile: 010-7434-3844

And also with a good image for the health,
Its spices and seasonings are prior to others, but it has put me
shame.
For all that, thinking it to be sorry,
I begin to trim the garlics to peel as our spices of our life,
After late evening with peeling its pieces and roots,
The weight of the garlics decreased in half size.
It is an error of our household not to be concerned about.
So things, decayed or sprouted newly,
Should sing a farewell song with a last letter,
Spring has come already under very nose.

- Tr. by Won Eung-Soon

통마늘을 까며

통통하던 근육이 쏘옥 빠졌다
오랜만에 건져 올려 지난해를 지낸 통마늘
나이가 든 것도 아닌데 얼굴이 야위고
근육이 쏘옥 빠졌다
가벼운 몸 끌어안고 맹물에 안겼다
물속에 몸을 채운 통마늘은
무심하게도 둥둥 떠 딴전을 보고 있다
질 좋은 마늘은 영양가 있고
건강에 좋은 이미지에 양념과
조미료감이 우선인데 부끄럼만 가득 찼다
그래도 안쓰러워 다듬고 벗기는 손짓
삶의 양념감 낮부터 생각다 못해
어둠이 진 후에야 쪽과 뿌릴 다듬으니
체중이 절반으로 줄었다
가족들이 너에게 무심했던 것이 죄다
온몸으로 몸부림치다
썩고 싹 난 놈은 할 수 없이 죄 없는
이별가를 부르고 편지를 써야만 했다
봄은 벌써 코앞에 다가왔다.

A Pear Flower

One day
Altogether
Being opened together with an outcry,

Without a sound of the footmark
Standing with a full-dress attire named moonlight on,
For what reason
Did you knock my window so much?

The full-dress attire
Trailing away
With an unripe pear's story left.....

Alas!
The fruits of outcry
Were hung as a lamp,
And were ripe densely.

- Tr. by Won Eung-Soon

Hyung Jong-hee/Korea

*A Reciter
*An Ex-Radio Actress of K,B.S.
*First Debut as a poet from "Hanmaek Literature"
*A Member of the Korean Writers' Association
*Director, the Society of the World Poetry
*A Member of "the Gangnam Literature"
*Registered in the great Dictionary of Korean poetry
*Joint Works of Poetry: "Stories at the Corner Coffee House" The Light of High-noon", etc.

배꽃

어느 날
일제히
함성으로 열리더니

발자국 소리도 없이
달빛 도포를 드리우고 서서
어쩌자고
나의 창문을 그토록 두드리셨나요

풋배사연 남겨 두고
멀어져 가는
도포자락……

오호라
함성의 그 열매
등불처럼 달렸어라
촘촘히도 익었어라.

The Cherished Desire in My Mind

You
Are buried under the lowest place,
I wish you would bloom like those wild flowers,
Always as white and clear as your smile.

Your young buds, opening shly,
Melting flower's dye stored away
Throughout the winter in every empty branch,
Are shaking with waiting as yet
Even in the cold wind,

Jang Dong-suck/Korea

*First Debut as a Poet in a Monthly Magazine, "The Korea Poetry"(2003) "The Korea Poetry", and as an Essayist in "Good Literature"(2006)
*Member of the Korean Writers' Association; of the Korean Poet's Association; of the Korean Essayist's Association
*Won an Author's Prize of this year from "The Good Literature"
*President of the Guro Branch of the Korea Writers' Association
*Won the Great Prize of the World Poetry
*(Present) Official of the Public Health Center
*Poetic Anthology:
*Your Image Glimmering in the Window
*A Soul Filling An Empty Space
*The Most Beautiful Exit
*An Aquarelle of Gurodong
*Man Exists in Loneliness
*Essay: In the Night with the Sun
*e-mail : stone2277@naver.com
*#67 Uhyeon-ro, Gangseo-gu, Gangseo Hill State Apt, 114-804
*Hand Phone: 010-5234-8907

Your breast, toward tomorrow
Has to be painful and sore,
As new and sweet
As opening hope's eyes in delight,

Hanging a piece of dream
On every flower petal,
And running toward the world
To spurt the deeper and purer hope
With your might shaped in passion,

You,
Even though shutting up into the wild weeds,
I wish you would live confidently like those wild flowers
With always a generous laugh.

- Tr. by Won Eung-Soon

염원

너희들은
가장 낮은 곳에 묻혀 있지만
언제나 해맑은 웃음으로
저기 저 들꽃처럼 피었으면 좋겠다

겨우내 품었던
빈 가지마다 꽃물을 풀어 헤쳐
수줍게 터트린 꽃망울들
아직은 기다림 속에
차가운 바람에 흔들릴지라도

내일을 향해
가슴이 아프고 저려야만
새롭고 향기롭게
환희에 찬 희망의 눈을 틔우듯

한 조각 꿈을
꽃잎마다 매달고
더 짙고 순결한 소망을 품기 위해
혼신을 다해 빚은 열정으로
세상을 향해 달려가는

너희들은
거친 잡초 속에 갇혀 있지만
언제나 넉넉한 웃음으로
저기 저 들꽃처럼 살았으면 좋겠다

A Cup

A shrewd you
With no arms,
But with only a muzzle and the buttocks,

You,
Who only is sitting with no breath,
Showing your true colors
onto the dark cupboard,

You,
Who desire to kiss approaching to the thirsty or to the peevish people,

---

Jeon Hong-gu / Korea

*Finished Dept. of Writing Creative Works, Art Graduate School, Jung-Ang Univ.
*First Debut as a Poet and Essayist from the Trend of Literature(1991).
*Member of the Korean Writers' Association, and of the Kuro Writers' Association.
*Director of the Christian Writers' Association of Korea, and Advisory Committee of Kookbo Literature.
*Poetical Anthology: "A Sound like Dog", "A Shed for a Melon Field", "The Sky Suspending on the Tree's Branch";
*Poetical Internet's Anthology: The No. 4th, "The Red Apple to the Core", The No. 5th, "A Rainbow in the Murky Clouds", The No. 6th, "For all that, Let's live Together"
*Awarding Prizes: Won the Excellent Prize from the Literary Trend Association, and a Main Prize from the National Race Literature of Korea, and Great Prize of Essay from Sejong Cultural Arts, *Won the Best Prize of the Public Subscription for the Handicapped in Nationwide Contest(2018), *Won the Main Prize of the Society of the World Poetry(2018)
*Won the Best Prize of the Public Subscription for the Handicapped in Worldwide Contest(2018), *Won the Great Prize of Literature from the Munhak Newspaper(The Korean Literary Newspaer)
*Address: [12045] Onam-eup, Yangji-ri, 105, Nam-Yangju City, Samshin Apt. 101-507. Korea.
*E-mail : yesnyes@hanmail.net *Mobile: 010-5290-6719.

Staying too long and when filled with your inside,
Soon waiting to be emptied, and being warped,
Or unmoved for a few days.

But, you,
If you got a chance,
Turning around to touch lots of lips,

You, being foolish,
Who don't feel your own breast hot or cold,
And with not feeling to like or to grumble,

You who are capricious,
With no relation to drink up clearly or to remain,
To pass round, to bump(hit),
But to desire to be kissed with lots of other people,

You,
Who are crafty and malicious,
Desiring to be loved from any one,
With having a buttock.

- Tr. by Won Eung-Soon

잔

팔은 없고
아가리에 궁둥이만 달린
맹랑한 너

어두운 찬장 속에서
숨소리도 내지 않고 앉아 있다가도
꺼내 주기만 하면 본색을 드러내는
너

목마른 사람에게나 토라진 사람에게 다가가
입맞춤 원하면서 엉덩이 비비고 있다가도
속을 채워 주면 금세 비워 주길 기다리기도 하고
픽 삐져서 며칠 끄떡 않을 때도 있는
너

그러다가도 기회만 오면
좌중을 차례로 돌며
입술 맞대는 너

가슴이 뜨겁거나 차갑거나
좋아하지도 투덜거리지도 않는
멍청한 너

말끔히 마시거나 남거나 돌리거나
부딪치거나 상관하지 않는데
다만, 돌려가며 키스해 주길 바라는
요망스러운 너

누구에게나
사랑받길 좋아하는
볼기 달린 요물인
너.

An Unknown Flower

I, an unknown flower,
Who am I? Nay, no one knows the flower,
Imitating a pretty flower's wat
Without appearance and fragrance,
But the bees and the butterflies came to me,
Day and night,
I, an unknown flower
Joining together with
Rain, wind, snowy cloud, sunlight, star light, and star light,
I am an unknown flower with no name
Having lived a little sadly in this world,
But now keeping on living in this world,
And always I am an unknown flower,
Who it will survive forever in this world.

- Tr. by Won Eung-Soon

Jeong Ji-ahn/ Korea

*Born in A-san city, Choongnam
*Works : 4th : One Year, Just 2013
5th : A Violent Gust Of Wind(2015. 4)
6th : Half Past Five In The Morning(2015. 5)
7th : Young-eun, Dream Drinker(2018. 7)
*Member : Literary Society Of The World Poetry, Korean Writer' s Association,
*International PEN in Korean Pen Club
*mail address : gongseri@hanmail.net

이름 모를 꽃

나, 이름 모를 꽃
누군가? 아니 아무도 알지 못하고
모양도 향기도 별것 없어
그저 예쁜 꽃 흉내나 내보는 꽃
그래도 벌과 나비는 곁에 와 주었고
낮이나 밤에
비 바람 눈 구름 햇빛 달빛 별빛
모두 함께 살아낸
나, 이 세상 약간 서럽게 무명으로 살아 온
이름 모를 꽃
나, 지금도 이 세상에 살고 있는
이름 모를 꽃
나, 이 세상에 영원히 살아있을
언제나 이름 모를 꽃

The Season with A Hydrangea

With my eye rims blushed
I dressed up again in flowery lamp.

If the lazy days
The sun was lying on the ridge line far away here,
Embrace the watery shadow dejectly in the breast,
Shall the fragrance be the butterfly's flapping?

The shy confession that I heard carelessly,
Is like a newly-married throbbing
Of my summer day over spreading here and there!

The lover's respiration hearing secretly,

The sweet wedding bouquet
Like a dream not returning!

The delicate smile
That is not filled far enough,
Let it spread out far far off!

- Tr. by Won Eung-Soon

Jeong Myeong-hee / Korea

*President of the Gyunggi Literary Forum
*Vice President of the Writers' Society at the Literature and Criticism
*Vice President of the Literary Man's Association at Gyunggi Literature
*Vice President of Suwon Poets' Association
*Vice Chairman of the Korea Story, Artist Associetion
*Representative Director of 'the Production of Happiness'
*Literary Works: Poetic Work: "Love, One Leaf & Yearning, One leaf"
Children's Verse: "Sunbeams in the Rain"
Juvenile Story: "The Rainbow my Mother Bought"

수국이 있는 계절

눈가에 볼웃음 달고
연보랏빛 꽃등불로 옷매무새 고쳐 입었다

멀리 보이는 능선 위로 햇빛 길게 누워
꼼지락거리는 날들
물그림자 너울 쓰고 초연히 품에 안으면
향기는 나비의 고운 날갯짓이련가

무심코 들어버린 수줍은 고백
여기저기 번져가는 내 여름날의
신혼 같은 설레임이여

나지막이 들려오는 님의 숨소리

돌아올 수 없는 꿈결
내 사랑의 향긋한 웨딩부케여

미처 채우지 못한 고혹스런
잔영의 미소
멀리 멀리 번져 나가라

Daybreak at Vientiane

Daybreak at Vientiane
Shines its good earth with a rose,
Since the black clouds covered its light
For many years.

People do not know the real well-being
Until they suffered a pain,
And so they do not know the real happiness,
Until they shed tears of lament.

Daybreak shines the gaps
Between the empty field of Vientiane,
The iced ground is melted,
The roses bloom in their breast.

The great sheets of rain without season
Was the life-giving water to wash these breasts?
The morning glow at Vientiane
Dawns as a burning fire.

- Tr. by Won Eung-Soon

Jeong Sook-ja / Korea

*First Debut through Hanwool Literature as a New Poet
*Graduated from Graduate School of Service Administration of Kyunggi Univ.
*Director, the Society of the World Poetry
*Won a great Prize from "the Lyrical Literature"
*Won a best Prize from members of the National Assembly
*Won a great Prize for Contribution to the Social Activity of the Popular Culture Arts
*A Manager of Ex-Youth Hostel
*Served as a Director of the Korean Cutural Arts for a General Alliance of Eligible Voters
*Served as a Director of the Steering Committee of the Literary Association for the Korean Pressman

비엔티안의 여명

먹구름 빛을 가린 지
비엔티안의 오랜 세월
여명은 장미를 싣고
대지를 비춘다

아픔을 겪어봐야
평안의 맛을 알고
서러움의 눈물 흘러봐야
행복 귀한 줄을 안다

비엔티안 벌판
사이사이 틴들 비치고
얼었던 땅은 녹아
가슴에 장미꽃이 피어난다

철없는 빗줄기
이 가슴 씻는 생명수였나
아침노을 타는 불빛
비엔티안에 동이 튼다.

A Mountain Plum

When the waters falling from a high waterfall shake silence,
The fruits are so green, April month! searching for so fast,
They learn to grow themselves in disregard of the weed's bitter
sound.

Though, to be a girl who want to meet you ardently,
I pull up a coat collar and make a muffler fly,
I heard to empty a throbbing mind in a moment.

When a wind blows violently, they say to me, 'open the stone gate',
And if being troubled, 'kiss your own cheeks'
And say again, 'remain only a good fruit with a gentle mente image.'

- Tr. by Won Eung-Soon

Jin Sang-soon / Korea

*Ex-Chairman of Writer's Association at Gimjae Branch
*President at General Society of Arts of Korean Painting
*Member of Literary Men's Association of Korea
*Vice President, the Society of the World Poetry
*Vice Chairman of Kirin Literature at Jeon-Buk
*Member of Literary Men's Association of Jeon-Buk
*A Compilation Committee of A Dictionary of Modern Poets in Korea
*Received Prizes: - Chosen Four Times at The Nation-Wide Arts Exhibition of Byok-Gol
- Won the Prize of new Poet from "The Han-Kook Poetry" monthly, Won the Great Prize from "The Han-Kook Poetry" monthly, Won the Prize of Culture of Gimjae Citizens, Won the Prize of Nosan Literature
*Publication: An Extra Star, Hanging in the Sky, The Reason the Wind Sits on the Tree, Now and Then, On Such A Day, Long Letters of A Crane

산매실

비폭에 떨어지는 물 고요를 흔들 때
그 열매 하도 푸러 섭적 다선 4월이여
잡풀의 쓴 소리 접고 제 홀로 크는 법을 배운다.

너를 만날 이유에서 간절한 소녀이고 싶어
바바리 깃 세우고 머플러 날리지만
한순간 설렘도 병인 양 비우라는 말 들었다.

바람이 섭슬릴 때 돌문을 열라 하며
무한정 괴롭거든 제 볼에 입맞춤하고
유순한 심상을 담아 정실만 남기라 한다

To Sprout a Little Dream

I budded one little dream
Seeming to pass, or to forget
After the time by the mind's anchor,
And my breast was moved
By one dream at childhood,
Flashing across my mind unexpectedly.

Not to lose you(dream),
Every time when my mind was delicate,
Taking out a little dream one by one to look,
You and I are united as one endlessly.

Though having unsatisfied feelings yet,
Compared to realizing all things,
The hours, flowing on after my mind
Sit together,
And sprout a little dream. again.

- Tr. by Won Eung-Soon

Jung Hyun-im/Korea

* Poet and Artist(Painter).
* Director of the Society of the World Poetry.
* Literary Man's Association of the Korea Race Literature.
* Awarding Prizes: Won the Main Prize of the Korea Race Literature. Won the Special Prize of Public Subscription for the Korea Woman's Fine Arts.
* Poetical Works: "A Small Island of the Afternoon", "I Won't Lament Any More", "I Would Like To Say 'Love You'", "A Little Dream As Being One"
* Address: #20(3rd Story), Unchi-ro No.100 gil, Buk-gu, Gwangju City, Korea.
* Mobile : 010-5642-7923
* E-mail: hyeonim9282@daum.net

작은 꿈 하나 되어

작은 꿈 하나 싹을 틔웠지
마음의 닻으로 시간 따라 흐르며
잊은 듯하다가
문득 문득 떠오르는
그 어릴 적 꿈 하나로
내 가슴은 흔들렸었지

너를 놓칠 수 없었기에
마음이 애잔해 질 때마다
작은 꿈 하나씩 꺼내어 바라보며
너와 나는 끝없이 하나가 되었지.

다 이루었다 하기엔
아직도 미진하지만
여기 이 자리,
나의 마음 따라 흘러온 시간들이
한데 모여 앉아
작은 꿈 다시 싹 틔워 보네

The Homecoming's Song

Into the forest along the edge of Sungtle's Peak,
A doleman was blacker,
Above the far sky of Mt. Bangzang,
Now I saw again
The rising fluff cumulus,
This is my old hometown that I never forget.

The water flowing from Mt. Munsoo valley
Makes the fields before the doleman,
And is flowing along the Incheon river for 5 thousand years.
The camellier flower at the Sunwoon temple is more crimson,
Now I saw again,
The hometown that I never forget even in my dream.

- Tr. by Won Eung-Soon

Kang Hee-Seok/ Korea

*Born in Gochang, Jeonbuk, Korea
*Discharged as a Navy Official
*Served in Daehan Aviation for 20 years
*Made a new Debut as a Poet from the Munye-Sajo, Monthly Magazine(2011)
*Poetic Anthology: 1st "I Killed a Cow"(2012)/ 2nd "The Song for Homecoming"(2014)
*(Present) Served as a Commentator for the Culture in Midang, Seo Jeong-ju Literature Center(Gochang)

귀향의 노래

성틀봉 기슭 따라 수풀 속
고인돌은 더욱 검었고
방장산 먼 하늘 위에
피어나는 솜털 뭉게구름
이제 나는 다시 보았네
세월 가도 잊을 수 없는 옛 고향

문수산 고랑에서 흐른 물
고인돌 들판을 적시고
인천강 따라 오천년을 흐르네
봄마다 선운사 동백꽃 더욱 붉구나
이제 나는 다시 보았네
꿈에서도 잊을 수 없는 그 고향

The Sound at Dawn

Do you see the dawning sound?

The deep shade of the sun
As if it doesn't reach its beginning yet,
All kinds of several birds' chirpings
Are decorating ins and outs of this country.

Until the present through Chosun since the founder of Korean nation Tangun,
This country has been a lamplight before a wind,
Always being in pain and danger like Mt. Baekdu with an active volcano,

Kang Young-duk/Korea

*First Debut as a Poet through monthly magazine <Munhak 21>in 1998
*Put my name on a Biographical Dictionary in 2002
*Put my literary work on the Biographical Encyclopedia
*Member of SGI Literary Man's Association
*Member of the Millennium Literary Society(Ex-General Secretary)
*Won the 31st Main Prize of the World Poetry.
*Joint Literary Works:
A Clamor; A String of Leaves;
Yearning becomes flower by the expression in your eyes;
The Wind that Brings Life.
*Poetic Anthology: "The Time's Channel"
*President : A Counselor lf a Welfare Society
*Address: 1-202, Daehan apt., 381-18, Hwagok1-dong, Gangseo-gu, Seoul, Korea
*E-mail: luxvia@naver.com
*Phone NO: 02-2604-8234 / 010-9970-8234

The hidden sound, feeling cramped more and more upon us,
In order to find for Pytoncjid at Mt. Baekwoon,
And find for a white birch wood at Wondae-ri, Inje,
Who can make a step forward?
And who can give out breath comfortably?

This country(Daehan) is emitting its true intention
Through our hundred thousands young people's groups
Concerning about state affairs,
Our banner of peace, safety, and development in one
Will blaze up in a flame.

Now can you hear the sound at down?

- Tr. by Won Eung-Soon

먼동이 트는 소리

먼동이 트는 소리 보이는가

아직 짙은 해그늘은
서막에도 미치지 않은 듯
온갖 잡새소리
나라 안팎을 장식하고 있구나

단군 이래 조선을 넘은 오늘날까지
바람 앞에 등불이요
활화산을 품은 백두산처럼
험난하고 위태롭지 않은 적이 없었지만
점점 옥죄이는 숨은 소리
백운산으로 피톤치드 찾으랴
인제 원대리 자작나무숲 찾으랴
뉘 먼저 휘두르랴
숨 한 번 편히 쉴 수 있겠더냐

국운을 염려하는
10만 청년 국사 육성 결집으로
대한이 사자후하노니
하나된 평화, 안정, 발전의 기치는
불길되어 일어서네
불국토 진미래 세세생생 지켜나가네

먼동이 트는 소리 이제 들리는가

A Round Truth

The reasonable fact the sun rises at east
And sinks at west is moved and thankful everyday.

If the sun rises at west and set at east,
It would be surprising and absurd troubles of universe.

If the earth and the heaven come in contact and turn round,
All things in the heaven and the earth would be only changed into
  soybeans flour.

There is a way that everyone could walk freely
On all the ground under the heaven.

Kim Chong-ki / Korea

*Born in Sun Cheon city(1938~)
*Graduated from Goryou Universty majoring on Korean Literature, pre-principal of Suong Eui Girls High School Korean Literature, presbyter of Korean Presbyterian Church, made a debut as a poet by 'Christian Literature' 'Trend of Literature' 'Modern Sijo'
*Member of Korean Literature Association, member of International PEN in Korean Branch, awarded by Young Rang Literature Prize, Christian Poet Prize, Trend of Literature Prize and Epipodo Literature Prize
*Director, the Society of the World Poetry
*Collections: As Sunrays in Vacant site (1991), Laugh Bunged up on End of Nose, Sorrow Always Living in My Mind, I'll Live Unreservedly and Gay-spiritedly, A star Alive in My Mind literary group magazine : High Jump Of Grasshopper, The clean person washing even though the tear
*Address : 621, Sanghadong, Giheunggu, Yongin City, Suwon-dongmaeul Ssangyong Apt. 303-1701, Geonggido, Korea.

The thing that the earth has no first and last of its way
Is the round truth that the earth is round,

Which Galileo Galilei proved at the risk of his life.

- Tr. by Won Eung-Soon

둥근 진리

해가 동녘에서 뜨고 서녘으로 지는
당연한 사실이 날마다 감동 감사다.

해가 서쪽에서 뜨고 동쪽으로 지면
황당하고 기겁할 우주적 번뇌일 게다.

땅과 하늘이 맞닿아 돌아가면
천지간이 물체가 콩가루 될 뿐이다.

하늘 아래 온 땅 위 곳곳에는
누구나 자유로이 다니는 길이 있다.

지구에 길의 처음과 끝이 없는 건
갈릴레이가 목숨 바쳐 명증(明證)한

지구, 둥글고 둥글다는 둥근 진리다

Sleets

My mind is so lonely,
When I look at the sky by chance,
The sleets are flown down from heaven.
I want to see
And to yearn urgent voices,
That lonesome dancing groups
Turning round the empty space,
What are they roaming for?
I wish that those many stories
Written in the grey sky
Would fall down as heavy snowfall
Clasping to their breast with one another.

- Tr. Won Eung-Soon

Kim Don-young / Korea

*Pen Name: Eunro. Born at Youngkwang, Jeonnam, Korea.
*Graduated from the Air and Correspondence College.
*First Debut as a Poet through "the Sinchoon Literary Arts" and "Literary Movement & Trend".
*Chief Editor, the Society of the World Poetry
*A Photo-Writer(Present).
*Won a Main Prize of the World Poetry.
*A Member of Literary Writer's Association of Korea.
*Poetic Anthology: "The Wind's Whisper"
* Address : Metrotower 2226, 856, Tongil-ro, Eunpyeong-gu, Seoul, Korea.

진눈깨비

내 마음 허허로워
문득 쳐다본 하늘에
진눈깨비 날린다
그립다 보고 싶다
다급한 목소리들
휘휘 허공을 도는
저 쓸쓸한 군무는
무엇을 찾아 헤매는가
회색의 하늘에 쓰는
저 많은 사연들
차라리 서로를 끌어안고
폭설로 내렸으면

A Weathercock

The tree leaves are gathered densely by the strong winds.
Truth is filled with smiles fully, the selfish desire is the poetical hour
Truth, goodness, beauty.
The escaping story
Is a hide and seek named the degenerated wave.

The sound of falling leaves in winds is one of tears performing for myself,
That is only to escape the wind with illogicalness of the 5 colors forgot,
Love
Sets out in a journey
In a thorough consistency.

- Tr. by Won Eung-Soon

Kim Dong-il/ Korea

*Pen Name: A-Song
*Born at Hongcheon, Gangwon-do, Korea
*Made a new Debut as a Poet from the Sijo Literature
*Member of Ganwon Sijo Association
*Member of the Korea Writers' Association
*Director, the Society of the World Poetry
*Member of the SijoPoets' Association
*(Present) Served in the Sijo Literature
*Won a Prize of a New Poet from Sijo Literature, in 2013.
*(Present):Chief Director of Shinkwang Procurement
*Address: (08289) Gongwon-Ro, 6 Na-Gil, Gugo-Gu, Seoul, Korea.
*Email: shinkwang88@hanmail.net *H.P: 010-6336-7870

바람개비

강풍에 나뭇잎들 옹기종기 모여 든다
진리는 미소 가득 사욕은 풍유 시간
진선미
회피 사연은
퇴화 물결 숨바꼭질

바람의 낙엽 소리 나 홀로 흥행 눈물
오색의 어불성설 잊은 채 바람막이뿐
사랑은
일사불란 속
여행길에 오른다

A Missionary's Dream(Vision)

I would have drawn and carved a dream
Into the engraved tree and the rock,
That had sent away into the sky as a folded paper.

I sent half a century
Turning over and over, talking in my sleep.

I responded with Amen
To thy summon
From the unfamiliar, half-done land.

Kim Eui-shik/Korea

*Born in Sangju,Gyeongbuk. Grown up Chungju
*Pen-name: Cheong-seok *Got Ph.D. of Administration
*Now serves concurrently as a professor at Hanyang Cyber University
*A Visiting Professor at a Graduate school of Administration, Dongguk University
*A lecturer at the Juvenile financial education centre
*(present) Serving as a Prof. of Invitation at Incheon University
*A director at Save zone I&C
*A director of Institute of managing the Global Green(present)
*A director at Korea Production Society
*Started a literary career through Literary Movement & Trend
*Director of International Diplomacy, the Society of the World Poetry
*Published poetical works entitled 'Becoming a root of a dandelion
*Professor of Life University of Business Administration in Combodia.
*Literary work entitled 'Pull an Oar When the Wind Goes Down', 'Live a wealthy man till Die', 'Hold the World in Your Bosom' and ten others.
* A Llecturer of the Graduate of Smaller Enterprise, Soongsil Univ,
* The Blue, Dreaming Stone
* Member of Writers' Association of Korea, of the Literary Meeting of Elders of Korea, of the World Poetry, of the Seijong Literary Meeting
*Address: 05301, 126gil 72, No.401(gildong) Yangjaedae-ro, Gangdong-gu, Seoul, Korea
*E-mail: huvac1004@hanmail.net *Caf addrees : Caf.daum.net/YesKim

Carving a seal in the bone,
Cutting deep into my heart,
Carving it on the tombstone of mind by help of the Lord' s blood,
After half century passed, the dream was achieved by Him,
It was realized by Him as I told and he heard it,
Through the help of divine providence,
Even though the dream was not seen and held by the hand
At the crossroad of life and death whether it was real or unreal,
His sound, "Ye, be still and know that I am God"
Was clear and new to me.

- Tr. by Won Eung-Soon

선교사의 꿈

종이 접어 창공으로
날려 보낸 꿈
조각목에 그려놓고 바위돌에 새겨둘 걸

반세기를 엎치락뒤치락
잠꼬대로 수 놓았네

설익고 낯설은 땅
부르심 따라
아멘하고 화답했네

뼈마디에 각인하고
골수에 채워
흘리신 피값으로 심비(心碑)에 새기니
반세기를 지나서야 이루어 주시네
말한 대로 들린 대로 이루어 주시네
주야로 중보하시는 손길 따라
보이지도 잡히지도 않은 그 꿈
꿈인지 생시인지 생사의 갈림길에서
너희는 가만히 있어 내가 하나님 됨을 알지어다
그 음성 더욱 새로워졌네

Her Yard

When I looked around her yard,
She
Left lonely
Making her way through the cold blowing wind,

Around this time last year,
She said,
'I am only a worker'
Raising her sharp voice,

Her red car was not seen
In the empty parking place,

Only the standing signboard for her gallery
Is fluttering in wind solitarily,

Kim Hye-sook/ Korea

*Member of Jeonju City Assembly
*Graduated from Graduate School of Jeonju Univ. Ph.D.
*Director of Leadership Center in Female Committee of the Democratic Unified Party
*Vice Chairman of Special Committee of Central
*Environment in Democratic Unified Party
*Served as a Visiting Prof.
*Mobile : 010-7736-1896
*E-mail : khs-ria@hanmail.net

Pushing the entrance door as usual,
To seek for her,

With the hard closed door not opened,
Only a few retrospects
Whirl me in my lonesome heart,

The only endless remorses
Keep flickering round
Her empty yard.

- Tr. by Won Eung-Soon

그녀의 마당

그녀의 마당을 둘러보니
불어오는 찬바람을 가르며
그녀는
쓸쓸히 떠나가고

작년 이맘때
'나는 그저 일하는 사람'이라며
칼칼한 목소리로
목청을 돋우던 그녀

휑하니 텅 빈 주차장에
그녀의 빨간 차는 보이지 않고

갤러리 입간판만이
덩그러니 바람에 나부끼는데

여느 때처럼 그녀를 찾아
출입문을 밀어보지만

굳게 닫힌 문은 열리지 않은 채
허전한 내 가슴에
하나 둘 추억만 맴돌고

하염없는 회한만이
텅 빈 그녀의 마당을
감돌고 있구나

The Back Side of the Moon

The wind, suffocated
By an entangled mind is rolling only its eyeball,
Stupidity! trying to remember
The bygone days to erase,

The yearning remained in the corner of the heart
Sits on the dry shoulders
Stirring up the flowing time.

Today
The pain's lump that embraced me
Hides over there in the rear of the moon
Rolling over between dusk
Losing its direction(course).

- Tr. by Won Eung-Soon

Kim Hyo-yeol/ Korea

*Representative Director of the Eulji Publishing Company
*Publisher of "An Encyclopedia of the Korean Poetry"
*Director of Financial Affairs, the Society of the World Poetry
*Address : #603. 41, Yanghwajin-gil, Mapo-gu, Seoul, Korea
*E-mail : ejp4050@hanmail.net
*Phone : 02-334-4050

달의 뒤켠

엉클어진 마음에
숨죽인 바람은 눈망울만 굴리는데
지워야 할 지난날을
기억하려는 아둔함이여

마음 한구석에 남아 있는 그리움은
흐르는 시간을 휘저으며
메마른 어깨 위에 앉는다

오늘도
날 껴안은 아픔의 덩어리는
어스름 사이로 뒹굴며
방향을 잃고
저만치서 달빛 뒤에 숨는다.

Capri Isle, As Your Lover

Your figure with Emerald Color,
A few pieces of dream that Capri embraces into the transparent light,
Make the present and future surging by its wing's flapping.

I
Am embraced in your blue breast
With my soul deprived,
And embark on a ship for a far, beautiful travel.

Capri!
Only by hearing its name, my heart feels nervous,
To become your lover without falling asleep,
I fall into a swoon
Sinking into your emerald light.

- Tr. by Won Eung-Soon

Kim Hyung-Ae/Korea

*Pen name: Cho-Woo *Poet, Essayist *She was born in Seoul.
*Director of Administrative Office in the Yonsei Medical Center.
*Delegate of Korea of WHO International Conference.
*Committee of the International Exchange Board of PEN, Korea Headquarter of the International PEN.
*Director of the Korea Christian Poet's Association.
*Director of the Essayist's Association of Korea.
*Vice President of the Writers' Society of the Chosun Lit.
*Awards: Great Prize of the 22th Essay Literature.
Great Prize of the 31st International PEN Club.
Main Prize of the 21st Youngrang Literature.
*Works: Poetic Anthology: My Pechka with Poems I). II).
*Essay Anthology: In the Pechka of my Mind. In the Pechka of my Soul.
In the Pechka of my Journey. In the Pechka of my Garden.

카프리, 그대의 연인되어

에메랄드빛 당신의 모습
투명한 빛 속에 품고 있는 꿈 조각들
현재와 미래를 날갯짓으로 출렁이네

나는
당신의 푸른 가슴에 안겨
영혼을 빼앗기고
아름다운 먼 여행길에 오르네

카프리!
이름만 들어도 설레이며
잠들지 못하는 당신의 연인이 되어
당신의 에메랄드빛 몸 속에 잠겨
혼절(昏絕)한다

카프리!
그대는 나의 영원한 연인이며
밀려오는 기쁨이어라

註: 이탈리아 남부 나포리 항에서 페리를 타고 카프리 섬으로 이동하여, 다시 모터보트,Blue Grotto를 타고 지중해의 진주라 불리는 카프리 섬의 절경을 둘러보았다. 푸른 동굴을 지나는데 그 빛은 에메랄드빛 보다 더욱 아름다웠다. 바위 주위에는 분홍빛 산호가 자라고 있었다. 그 황홀함에 빠져 헤어나지 못하고, 귀국하여서도 지중해의 그 푸른 바다가 눈앞에서 출렁이고 있다.

One Day of Discrepancy

Today
Is
Another happy day
In my life.

But

Today
Is
Another sad day
In my life.

That
Today is sad or happy
To me,
What is the reason?

- Tr. by Won Eung-Soon

Kim Jae-Myeoung/ Korea

*Born in Dangjin, Chungnam, 1962.
*A Pastor(Sinkwang Mehtodist Church, Chunan, Chungnam)
*Member of the Literary Society of the World Poetry
*Address: No. 77-17, Yonggok-dong, Chunan City, Chungnan, Korea(in Sinkwang Methodist Church)
*E-mail : kjm1210@hanmail.net
*Tel : 010-7522-8299

모순의 하루

오늘은
내 생애
또 하나의
행복한 날이었습니다.

한데

오늘은
내 생애
또 하나의
슬픈 날이기도 했습니다.

오늘이
내게
슬프고 기쁜 것은
무슨 까닭일까요?

The Eyeballs

The morning dewdrops
Formed in the blue eyeballs
Of the blue roe deer,
Are faded in the bright sunlight,

The thing
Remained
In the blue eyeballs
Vanished like the morning dewdrops,
Is only
An old white retrospect.

When
Lots of the old dew-laden mythology
Are gathered and scattered again,
The beautiful retrospect
Formed in the blue eyeballs
Of the blue roer deer,
Is only burning.

- Tr. by Won Eung-Soon

Kim Ji-yeul/Korea

*Graduated from The College of Chemistry in Joseon University.
*Finished The Graduate School of Jeonnam University(master of science) and that of Catholic Medical College(doctor of medicine).
*A professor of Jeonnam Medical College.
*The president of The Korean Nuclear Medicine Academy(1996~1998)
*Address : Myeong Jin Castle 102-304, 29, Yeonyang-ro 67beon-gil, Buk-gu, Gwangju, Korea

눈망울

청노루의
파아란 눈망울에 맺힌
아침 이슬은
찬란한
햇살 속에 감추어지고

아침
안개처럼
사라진
파아란 눈망울에 남은 것은
하얀
옛 추억일 뿐

이슬에 잠긴
숱한
옛 신화가
모였다 다시 사라지면
청노루의
파아란 눈망울엔
아름다운 추억만이
불타고 있다.

We are the Souls Traveling the Universe

Leaving the sky of universe that is far far away endlessly,
Passing by the iced country that is driving with a snowstorm,
Over the dangerous mountains wrapped in flames,
And here in a garden passing where the clouds covered the sun's face,
I, dressed in light, stand waiting for you,
Whom I have not seen once, and your clean-cut name
That I have heard of once,
Come on quick, say to me,
How bright my dress is,
And before the darkness swallows your dress of light.

We are the souls travelling a universe from a star to stars,
Say to them, a word being linked from a life to the next one,

Kim Jong-hee/ Korea

*Debut as a poet in Poetry Monthly' Magazine, 1982.
*Poetic Anthology : Until the last Day of the World, The Stone into Water, Beyond the Time, Madam S Falls Down, I Am Very Far Away, The Light and the Dark.
*A Director of The Literary Women's association, International pen club.
*The prize of Poetic Literature from the Poetry(Monthly Magazine), The prize of Christians Literature, The Great prize of Young-rang Literature.
*Won the great prize of the 31st Poetical Literature of the World Poetry
*Address : Messenapolice Rm.1202, No. 102. 45, Yangwha-ro, Mapo-gu, Seoul, Korea
*E-mail : gongpoem@hanmail.net
*H.P : 010-5229-0264

To bring it from a star to pther stars,
And say the word, say it to me,
Which I didn't say what I had not understood,
And that is confined in me,
By out of feeling what it means it yet.

That gloomy side, where the sun also does not shine,
Like the iced lumps
Ransacking through the cold space between stars,
Say to me,
Not to revolve endlessly as a blind star.

- Tr. by Won Eung-Soon

우리는 우주를 여행하는 영혼들

끝없이 멀고 먼 우주의 하늘을 떠나
눈 폭풍 몰아치는 얼음나라 지나서
불길 치솟는 험준한 산맥을 넘어
구름이 해의 얼굴을 쓸고 지나가는 여기
동산에서 나, 빛의 옷 입고 서서 기다리니
한 번도 본 적 없는 당신
한 번도 들은 적 없는 이름의 깨끗한 당신
속히 오셔요, 와서 말 해줘요
어둠이 빛의 옷 삼켜버리기 전에
내 옷이 얼마나 빛나는지를

우리는 별에서 별로 우주를 여행하는 영혼들
한 생에서 다음 생으로 이어지는 말
별에서 별로 가져가야 할 말을 말해줘요
그리고 내가 말하게 해줘요
아직 그것이 무엇인지 알지 못해 하지 못한 말
아직 그것이 무엇인지 느끼지 못해
내 안에 갇혀있는 말을

태양빛도 비추지 않는 어두운 저 편
별들 사이의 차가운 공간을 휘젓고 다니는
얼음덩이들처럼
눈먼 별이 되어 끝 모를 공전을 하지 않도록
내가 말하게 해줘요

A Grain of Vitamin C

The remote place, taking pains
Day and night, whether I will go or not,
The yesterday that I got on a plane,
Driven by a dubious thinking to go for the place again,

One moment thankful for
What I come to definite decision,
I draw my sons waiting above the cloud blindedly.

The son, being 40 years old more, free from vacilation,
"Mother, very hard for coming a long way here.

Kim Jeong-won/ Korea

* Graduated from English Dept. of Yonsei University, and from a graduate School of Education in Yonsei University, and from a graduate School of Myongji Univetsity
* Made first Debut as a Poet in The Literature Monthly.
* Collection(Anthology) of Poems:<Washing cold Hands>, <Pilgrim of Time>, <You were a Flower in other Heaven>, <Place of Emptiness>, <The late Autumn's Sunlight is very Warm>, The Anthology, <The life's Fin>, <The Alter Ego> tr. by Won Eung-Soon in Korean-English>, and <A Group Counselling, tr, by Kim Jeong-Won>, etc.
* Served as a Lecturer at Seongkyunkwn University and Myeongji University
* Won a Prize of Yulmok Literature, of Race Litetature, of Sowol Literature
* Member of Korea Pen in International, and Korea Writer's Association of Society of the Mirae Poets, Member of the Christian Writer;s Association of Korea, Director of Society of Female Literature of Korea
*Address : Hillstate 1103-804, 147, Pangyo-ro, Bundang-gu, Seongnam-si, Gyeonggi-do
* E-mail: wooajnee@hanmail.net

Ah, take it, ---",
A grain of Vitamin C he put in my mouth to soak,
Made me be moved to tears,

"When you are 5 years old,
I put it so in your mouth."

The son has laughed like a naughty boy,
And it's so good for me to call only his name.

- Tr. by Won Eung-Soon

비타민 C 한 알

순서바꿔야

갈까 말까 그 먼 곳
밤낮으로 바뀌던 생각
언제 또 다시 갈 수 있겠나 싶어
비행기에 올랐던 어제

결단을 내린 내게
고맙기도 한 순간은 구름 위
눈 감고 아들의 기다림을 그린다

불혹을 훌쩍 넘은 아들,
"어머니 머언 길 힘드셨지요
아앗 하세요, 이거…",
입안에 넣어준 비타민C 한 알
스며스며 눈시울 뜨겁더라

"네가 다섯 살 즈음 때
내가 그렇게 입 안에 넣어줬지"

아들은 여태 장난꾸러기같이 웃고
난 그의 이름만 불러도 그저 좋았다

The River of Exile's Place

Toward the red sunset,
Being opposite to the dazzling West River
Standing aside to its edge,
I look back on my days giving a deep bow upon knees.
Across the river of memory named
That has roamed about into thin fog through all night,
Bisul-trees, oak trees, mulberry trees of mountain, maple trees,
  Wormwoods, and eularias between silvery white birches,
Also put the finishing touches on their lives with ecstatic light,
And the silent river has been passing
Over thousand, ten thousand mountains.
The burning metaphors with soul' s fire
Into the red-colored sunset
About the edges of dry leaves
That have carried out their flowers, leaves, and fruits
Erase even the boundary of light and darkness.

- Tr. by Won Eung-Soon

Kim Mi-Rae/ Korea

*New Debut as a Poet with a New Poet's Prize from the Munyesajo, 1990.
*Served as Vice President of the Dongbaek Literary Society, and Seocho Literary Society, etc.
*Poetic Anthology: 'The Low Voice of Prizm', 'The Beautiful Time Travel', Joint Work: 'A Watchman of Dawn', 'The Lost Present Address', etc.
*Awarding Prize: 'The Main Prize of the Freedom Poetry', 'The Prize of Literature from the Hangeul Lit. and from the Seocho Society of Lit.', etc.
*(Present): Reciting Poet of the Literary Society of the Korean Writers, Member of the House of Literature, Director of the Seocho Literary Society.
*Address: (06544) Sinbanpo-Ro, Seocho-Gu 270, No. 103-1903

유배지의 강 9
-서강별곡

해 질 무렵
눈부신 서강* 마주하고
변방으로 비켜 앉아
무릎 꿇어 조아려 온 날들을 뒤돌아본다
밤새 물안개 속 뒤척이던
기억의 강을 지나
강 건너
은빛 자작나무 숲 사이 비술나무, 굴참나무, 산뽕나무도
돌단풍, 쑥부쟁이, 억새도
한 생을 황홀한 빛으로 갈무리하고
천산 만산 저 너머
침묵의 강 지나고 있다
꽃도 잎도 열매도 다 내어준
마른 나뭇가지 끄트머리에
자줏빛 노을 속
혼불로 타오르는 은유들이
빛과 어둠의 경계마저 지운다.

* 서강: 강원도 영월군 영월읍 방절리 단종 임금님의 유배지 청령포를 끼고 흐르는 강. 합수부에서 동강과 만나 남한강으로 흐른다.

A Pencil

Old mother in her nineties
Eagerly awaits every Tuesday.
When an old teacher teaches Hangeul
At the village senior's house.

About eighty years ago, she might have learned
Giyeok, Nieun, Digeut.

A letter to her grandson entitled her
To receive an excellence award with a certificate and a dozen
of pencil,
Which she brages about with a bright smile.

Until a bunch of tender love,
Handed by a wrinkled hand of the one
Who enjoyed learning for all her life,

Become stubby pencils of twelve,
Could she meet a myriad of new days humming,
Would I pray.

- Tr. by Kim Cheol-soo

Kim Seung-hwan / Korea

*First Debut as receiving a new Poet's prize from the quarterly magazine<the Munhak-Chunchoo>, and a new Essayist's Prize from the monthly <the Pure Literature>
*Vice President of the Kwangju Commission, and Director of the Korean Headquarter, International PEN.
*Vice President of Jeonnam Literary Man's Association/ *Director of Jeonnam Poet's Association
*Director of the Pajoo Branch, the National Agricultural Co-operative Federation(NACF)
*Prizes: Won the Prize of "the Jeonnam Literature", Won the great Prize of the Naju Culture and Arts, Won the Prize of the Arts and Culture from the Korea General Arts and Culture
*Literary Works: Poetical Anthology: <The Vicars' Valley Market of Recollection. *Essay Anthology: <A Dialogue with Natural Stones>
*Address: (58244) #76-8 Daho-Gil, Daebang Nobleland 110-604, Naju City, Jeonnam, Korea

연필

구순의 노모는 매주 화요일을
손꼽아 기다린다
마을 노인정에서 할아버지 선생님이
한글 가르치는 날

팔십여 년 전쯤에 쓰기 시작했을
기억 니은 디귿

증손자에게 쓴 편지가
우수상 되어 상장과 연필 한 다스를
선물 받았다고 환한 얼굴로 자랑하신다

평생 배움을 즐겨하던
주름진 손등으로
살며시 건네준 사랑 한 다스

열두 자루 몽당연필 될 때까지
콧노래 흥얼거리며
무수한 새날 품기를 기도한다

City

City is a dark-grey mosaic
Pressed down with stone and iron.

A child spills ink by mistake,
Letting a river flow-
A river the color of emerald.

Kim Won-gil/ Korea

*Born at Andong, Korea(1942)
*First Debut as a new Poet from the Poetic Part of "the Monthly Literature"(the Wolganmunhak)(1971)
*Recognized as a Professor of Poetics from Judging of Dept. of Education(1974
*The last Poetic Anthology in 2012 is translated in English, Japanese, France, Chinese language by the people of the country
*(Present) Served as a Manager of "the Society of the Creative Works"
Address: #427 Jiraeyesulchon-Gil, Imdong-Myun, Andong-Gun, Kyungbuk, Korea

도회

도회는 돌과
쇠로 눌러 박은
암회색 모자이크

아이가 잘못
잉크를 쏟아
에메랄드 빛 강이 흐른다.

A Confession

When darkness falls down,
I leave home
With a cold breast without the sunlight.

I mix well the free salutations
Under the vague light,
The grave everyday life of today,
And the hard, hot confessions to say
At the rate of gold.

And also mixing our superior's nagging,
An incredible lottery's hope,
An adverse reaction of medicines for depilation(alofecia),
And a scarlet gum concealed in her smile

Kim Young-sun /Korea

*Born at Soul/ Graduated from Electronic Telecomunication Engineering, Inchun Univ.
*Graduated from Dept. of the Creative Writing of Art and Literature, Graduate School, Jungang University, Seoul Korea.
*Member of the Society of the World Poetry
*Member of the Story Writers' Association
*A Painting & Poetry of Coterie with A Slop
*"Your Dominion", "A Sound of a Bamboo Flute", and "The Sonnet of Reubrong" in Coterie Magazine are inserted.
*Poetic Anthology: "A Yard the Poetic Aroma is Springing", by Joint Work
*Address: Jangan-dong, 111-8, Jungheung Building, 5Floor, Nanyum Music.Dongdaemun-Gu, Seoul, Korea

With all gassips of the unreliable world
To make a bubble with golden colour,
And to enjoy a burning taste for a throat.

The deep confessions
So as to enjoy them...

That the world is beautiful or sad,
The world is beautiful or sad,
That the world is sacred or cruel,
The world is sacred or cruel,

Confessing,
The life
Is beautiful or sad,
Beautiful, or cruel.

고백

어둠이 내리자
빛도 사라진 서늘한 가슴
길을 나선다

희미한 불빛아래
빗장을 풀어헤친 인사들
엄숙했던 오늘의 일상과
차마 하지 못한 뜨거운 고백들을
황금비율로 잘 섞어 담는다

갈구어대는 상사의 잔소리와,
똥 꿈을 믿고 산 복권의 희망과,
먹고 있는 탈모 약의 부작용과,
미소 속에 비친 그녀의 선홍빛 잇몸과,
얄팍한 세상에 모든 가십을 섞어
금빛도 찬란한 거품을 만들고
터질 듯 톡 쏘는 앙칼진 목 넘김을 즐긴다

즐긴 만큼
짙어가는 고백들...

세상은 아름답거나 혹은 슬프거나
사랑은 아름답거나 혹은 슬프거나
세상은 성스럽거나 혹은 잔인하거나
사랑은 성스럽거나 혹은 잔인하거나

고백하건대
인생은
아름답거나 혹은 슬프거나
성스럽거나 혹은 잔인하거나

Weeds

A peasant,
Sitting on the ditch of the wildly grown grass field,
Draws a deep breath.
He calms his mind hardly falling down to the bottom
That he made havoc of farming in the crops.
And it seems that the shivering sound of weeds is heard to the roots.
The weeds are taken out indiscreetly by his strong hands,
They are howling as heart-rending
And catching a glimpse at their birthplace.
It is due to our fault.

Ko Bang-kyu / Korea

*Born at Okjeri, Sungnaemyun, Gochang, Jeon-Buk, Korea
*Graduated from Dept of Literary Art of Masan Changshin University.
*Recommended As a new Sijo Poet from the Sijo Literature, 2003.
*Member of the Korean Writers' Association, of The Literary Coterie 'Soorim'
*Director of Management, the Society of the World Poetry
*Vice President of the Gochang Literature
*President of the Masan Branch of the new Age Literature
*Won the Great Prize of the World Poetry
*Poetical Anthology: <A Love As Rose Flower>.
*Won the new Poet's Prize of the Cultural Arts
*Won a Literary Work's Prize of the new Age Literature
* Won a Prize of a Chungma Writing Contest Over Whole Country
* Address: 463 Okje-ri,Sungnae-myun, Gochang-gun, Jeonbuk, Korea
* Tel. 063-562-3358/ 010-8559-1616
* E-mail: kbg461227@hanmail.net
* Daum Cafe: http://cafe.daum.net/kbg1227

The medical book, *Dong-Ui-Bo-Gam says the weeds are a good herb
More than a Jinseng.
So they complain feebly
Wishing to be given hospitable treatment some time.

- Tr. by Won Eung-Soon

*Dong-Ui-Bo-Gam(東醫寶鑑) : It's a medical book which was compiled as materials for the medical treatment of China and Korea in Chosun Dynasty.

잡초

농부는
무성이 풀 자란 밭 어귀에 힘없이 앉아
기-인 한숨을 쉰다
농사를 망쳤다며 썩어 문드러지는
마음 기둥을 간신히 잡는다
벌벌 떠는 잡초
떨리는 소리가 뿌리까지 들린다
억센 손에 무지막스레
뽑혀나간다
찢겨질 듯 울부짖는 잡초
곁눈질로 태어난 곳을 슬픈 체
힐끗 바라보고 있다
무지(無知)해서 그러지
*동의보감에는 인삼보다
더 좋은 약초라 한다
언젠가는 한번쯤 귀한 대접으로 살아봤으면
힘없이 푸념을 한다

The Snowy Day

Before it's very far-off distance,
It's the day good enough
To hold the man by the sleeve
Turning his back to go.

Even if
He tears himself away,
It's very lucky day,
Because I don't feel sorry or unkind.

The sound of footsteps growing distant
Scattered the snow with being crunchy,
It's rather
A thankful day.

Kou Sun-ja/ Korea

*Member of the Korea Pen Club, International Pen Club
*Director of the Public Information in the World Poetry
*Director of the Poetry Section in the Guro Writers' Association of Korea.
*The Literary Coterie of "The People Writing Poems".
*Committee of Lyrical Literature in the Korean Writers' Association
*Member of Promoting the Peaceful Unification of the Korean Race
*Won the Prize of Poetic Literature of the World Poetry
*Won the prize of the Creative Literature of Korea.
* Poetic Anthology : The Flower's Story, An Electronic Book, etc.
* Address: 1st floor, 14-194 Gonghan-dong, Kangseo-gu, Seoul, Korea
* Mobile Phone: 010-4742-8545
* E-mail: ksjmomo@hanmail.net

Unsweetened regrets
Always follow up,
But it's not too much for me to do,
It's a good day to walk all the way.

It's a good day to cry more than enough,
For me to look up
The flying snowflakes highly in the sky,
Though being suffused with tears.

- Tr. by Won Eung-Soon

눈 내리는 날

등 돌려 가는 이
아주 멀어지기 전
소맷자락 붙잡아도
될 성싶은 날이다

설령
뿌리친다 해도
야속하고 민망할 일 없으니
참 다행스러운 날이다

멀어지는 발소리
사락사락 흩어 놓으니
차라리
고마운 날이다

담백하지 못한 미련
자박자박 뒤따라도
하나 힘겨울 것 없으니
마냥 걸어도 괜찮은 날이다

눈물 나도
하늘 높이 날아오른 눈송이
올려다볼 수 있으니
맘껏 울어도 좋은 날이다

Life and Inheritance

All things in the world
Have lived and passed away
Through spring, summer, autumn and winter.

Don't cry,

Love also was born,
Ends away
Growing up with much trouble
Passing through spring, summer, autumn, and winter.

- Tr. by Won Eung-Soon

Koo Myong-sook/ Korea

*Graduated from Sookmyung Woman's Univ. and Graduate School of the same Univ.
*Graduated from Villevelt Univ. Germany. Ph.D. of Literature.
*New Debut as a Poet from "Poetic Literature" 1999. & "Poetry and Poetics" 2009.
*Won the Excellent Prize of Manhae 'Nym' and of 'Poetry and Poetics'
*(Present)
Emeritus Professor of Sookmyung Woman's Univ.
President of the World Society of Korean Language and Literature,
of the Society of Literary Man's of 'Poetry and Poetics'
of the Glocul(?)Woman's Network(Ltd.),
Vice Director of Seocho Cultural Center,
Director of the Sihwa Publication of Books
*Poetic Anthology: <Did She Cook Rice and Come With Some Raw Rice?>, <Walking>, <The Task We Live>, <The Heaven's Tree>, <The Makeups of Flowers>, <You, Pieta>

삶과 유산

세상의 모든 것들은
봄, 여름, 가을, 겨울을
살다 간다

울지 마라

사랑도 태어나선
봄, 여름, 가을, 겨울을 겪으며
힘겹게 자라나선
죽는다

The Place Where I Will Go To Rest

It's a lonely autumn.
For a soul with an empty, vacant breast, who has roamed without the place to go,
Autumn is called a man's season, so the loneliness is chilled to the marrow.
Climbing up the Daechung peak to fill a vacant breast with something on the desolate fall,
I wander over a wood-path with cone pine trees of Mt. Keumbyeong and white birches of Inje, Gangwon-Do.

I yearn the warm hand that it is grasping softly
The breast to stick out and the hand to thrust.
Where is the hand to catch as a kind companion
To talk to as becoming same party?

Kwon Young-e/ Korea

*Graduated from Dept of Public Administration, College of Politics and Law, Yonsei Univ.
*Officer of the 7th Regiment, ROTC of Korea
*Operative Committee of "the Consciousness of Literature"(Poet/ Essayist)
*Chief Editor of "the Korea Literature"
*Adviser of "the Saehan-Ilbo(daily newspaper)"
*Member of "the Seocho Literary Man's Association
*Director of "the Literary Society of the World Poetry"
*Prizes: Won the great Prize of Literature from Top-Leaders of Korea
*Address: #37 gil 20, Kwanak-ro, Dong-A Apt. 202-2303 Kwanak-gu, Seoul, Korea

There was a spring season to sprout and the time to go alone with a strong sun to me.
Bravely I came here, came joyfully with you by the hand,
Pushing aside through the dark shadow and high waves now at a time of finishing touches.

- Tr. by Won Eung-Soon

내가 쉬어갈 곳

외로운 가을이다
마음 허허롭고 텅 비인 가슴에 갈 곳 몰라 방황하는 영혼
가을은 남자의 계절이라더니 뼛속까지 외로움 져며든다
텅 빈 가슴 뭔가 채워보려 쓸쓸한 가을 날 대청봉 오르고
금병산 잣나무숲길 강원도 인제 자작나무 숲길 헤맨다

가슴을 내어 주고 내어 민 손 살갑게 잡아 주는
따사로운 그 손이 그립다.
언제나 내 편이 되어 살가운 말벗이 되어 주는
잡아 주는 손 어디 없을까

싹을 틔운 봄도 있었고 강열한 태양같이 홀로 갈 때도 있었다.
이제 갈무리 할 시간에 어둔 그늘과 험한 파도를 헤치고
여기까지 용감하게 왔는데 그대 손잡고 기쁨으로 왔는데

쓸쓸한 이 가슴 보듬어 줄 그 푹신한 가슴 그 손이 그립다
그 예비 된 동산 내 쉬어 갈 곳에 잘 견디고 잘 왔노라고
손 잡아줄 부드러운 손이 그립다 그 푹신한 가슴이 그립다

A Soliloquy

I have run looking at the front,
Turning back,
There stands a middle-aged man
Amid a balance weight,

As a bull ruminating nothingness
Of the bygone time and tide.

The high wall of the unlimited competition
Feels so dizzy even to see blankly,
Why the knapsack, packed on the back
Is so heavy,

Lee Byung-seok / Korea

*Pen-name: Deokwon
*Born at Daejeon City, Korea
*Director of the Society of the World Poetry
*Won a Prize as a New Poet from the Litetary Movement and Trend
*Won an Excellent Prize of the Literary Movement & Trend
*Won the Elegant Prize of the World Poetry
*Ph.D. of Management of Administration at Hannam University
*President of Samil Industry Co, Ltd.
*M&S Mentoring of Representative Director
*APEC Counselor
*Joint Representative of Volunteering Service Union
*Collection of Poems: Emitting the Romantic Fragrance
*Address : 1018, Daecheong Tower, 623, Gaepo-ro, Gangnam-gu, Seoul
*Mobile : 010-3681-5884
* E-mail : 31ind@naber.com

Shall I take measurements with a ruler
How much the itinerary distance would be remained?

Now I shall live with taking down all things,
In frequent breaks,
And shall live enjoying myself
Free from worldly cares.

- Tr. by Won Eung-Soon

독백

앞만 보고 달려왔다.
뒤돌아보니
추 안에 웬 낯선
중년남자 하나 서 있다

날아가 버린 세월의 무상함을
되새김질하는 황소처럼

무한 경쟁의 높은 벽은
태산처럼 보기조차 어지럽고
짊어진 배낭은
또 왜 이리 무거운지

남은 여정 얼마인가
잣대로 재볼까

이제는 모든 것 내려놓고
쉬엄쉬엄
노닐며 살리.
노닐며 살리.

Grass Flower

It hangs their heads down
For shaming itself to see a heaven,
The generous and quiet temper of grass
Growing as a low posture caused to open a world.

Its hard will and chastity resisting harsh trials,
Though it is tender and slender, was a feeble gesture
To keep its own chastity
And a struggle for its existence.

Lee Chang-soo/Korea

*Pen name: Dongjae
*First Debut as a Poet from the Part of poetry the monthly Magazine "Chosun Literature, and from Hiku Poetry of the quarterly magazine of "The Wilderness Literature"
*Director of the Klrea Headquarter, Internation PEN.
*Director of the Literary Society of the World Poetry.
*The Chairman of the Screening Committee in Public Writng Contest of 'Love of Filial Piety lf the Han Race'
*Served as an English Lecturer.
*Honor President of Dongdaemun Writers' Association and a Chief Editor of the literary magazine of "the Wilderness".
*Director of the Korea Modern Poets' Association and of the World Poetry Society.
*Member of the Korea Writers' Association.
*Won the Prize of the Head of Graduate School of Arts,. and of President of Jung-Ang University.
*Won the Main Prize of the Maewoldang Literature.
*Poetical Works: "The Winter Island", "Reclining on the Wind's Wall", etc.
*Joint Literary Works: "A World the Poetry Dreams", and others 6 vol.
*E-mail : saltis 46@hanmail.net

You are a graceful, pure and small grass flower
Combined with modesty and virtue,
Not with arrogance and vice,
Even harassed by all trialss and the rough-and-tumble of life.

Whom have you hated, reproached and wrangle with?

You are a gesture to inspire the wild and dangerous world
By your fragrance, enduring all the troubles and trials
To bloom flowers,
In spite of vexing all the pains.

- Tr. by Won Eung-Soon

초화(草花)

하늘을 보기가 부끄러워 고개를 들지
못하고
항상 낮은 자세로 살아가는 풀의 너그럽고 차분한
성품이 세상을 열어가는 단초가 되었네

여리고 가냘프지만 모진 풍파에 꺾일 줄 모르고
저항하는 굳은 의지와 절개는 순결을
지키려는 연약한 손짓이며 생존을 위한
몸부림이었네

그대 교만한 적 없고 악덕을 저지른 적 없는
겸손과 미덕을 갖춘 어질고 순한 작은
풀꽃이었네
온갖 고초를 다 겪으면서 세파에 시달려도

그 누굴 미워하거나 원망하거나 다투어 본 적 있었던가?

꽃을 피우기 위해서 곤경과 시련을 그대로
참고 견뎌내며 아픔도 서리어 있으련만
거칠고 험한 세상에 향기로 감화하려는 내솟는
몸짓이었네

In Darkness at Dawn

The world at dawn
Where I opened eyes by the raining sound
Is concealed from thick darkness
And sunk into deep silence.

The sound of a wall clock
Striking my hours to pass hastily
That opens freely into ears
At odd moments,
Disturbs my clumsy repose
Staying near the pillow,

An unwelcome visitor who visited at midnight
Beating at the window,
Knocks the mind's window
To make my notion wonder in darkness.

Lee Eui-young / Korea

*Born ar Paju, Geonggi-do, Korea
*First Debut as a new Poet from "the Baedusan Literature"
*President of the Literary Society of "the Geulpin-sam", *Vice President of the Seocho Literary Society, *Director of the Korean Writer's Regiment of Literature, *Director of the Literary Society of the World Poetry, *Managing Committee of The Modern Poet's Association of Korea,
*Prizes: Won the Prize of the Baekdusan Literature,
Won the Prize of the Seocho Literature
*Poetical Works: "A Wayfarer's Mind", "A Rhapsody of any Grass Flower"

To get up and make a light is only a mind,
Thinking of mine,
Squeezed by the turning heavy pressure,
Also is running,
But my body doesn't move any more.

- Tr. by Won Eung-Soon

새벽 어둠 속에서

비가 오는 소리에 눈을 뜬 새벽
세상은
짙은 어둠에 묻혀
깊은 침묵에 잠겨 있다

시나브로 열리는 귓속으로
매어있지 않은
나의 시간이 총총히 지나고 있음을 알리는
벽시계 소리가
베개 가에 머물던
어줍은 안식을 휘젓고

창문에 부딪히는
한밤에 찾아 온 달갑지 않은 방문자가
마음의 창을 두드려
상념(想念)이 어둠 속을 방황케 한다.

일어나 불을 켜야겠다는 것은 생각뿐
무겁게 누르는
회전하는 중압감에
생각은 달리는데
몸은 천근이다.

We Together

Let's go together subtracting heave burdens,
Breaking down the castle of evil conducts,
Building the house of good deeds,
And let's bloom flowers of love.

Let share together lots of many ideas,
Finding new happiness to touch a little,
Making it a friend of love as constance,
And let's appreciate it and keep on living.

Though we cannot catch the years together,
Leaning on our mind, and rubbing our backs warmly together,
Sending the declining sunlights,
Embracing the red morning glow,
Let's make our youth abundant,
Keep on going.

- Tr. by Won Eung-Soon

Lee Gyu-ik/Korea

*Born at Wooljin, Kyeonbuk, Korea
*First Debut as a New Poet through "the Literary Movement & Trend(2004)
*A Songwriter of the Music Copyright Association of Korea(1989)
*Chairman of the Literary Coterie "Seolpa Poetry"
*Member of the Society of the Korea Race Literature
*Director, the Society of the World Poetry
*(Present) Serving at Jeongpyeong Transportation
*Broadcasted "My Way" with 6 Poems by SBS Radio, "In Romantic Age"
*Poetic Collection: "he Snow-flower Dyed by the Sunset"
*Joint Work: "The City of An Alien"
*Address: #76 Deokyang-gu, Goyang city, Kyunggi-do, Samtermaeul 1st danji Apt. (No.103-1603), Korea
* E-mail : le0612love@naver.com * HP: 010-7156-4100

우리 함께

우리 함께 무거운 짐 덜고 가요
악행의 성을 허물고 선행의 집 지어
사랑의 꽃 피워가요

우리 함께 많은 생각 나눠가져요
조금씩 와 닿는 새로운 행복이 뭔지
여일 같은 사랑 친구 벗 삼아
조금씩 음미하며 살아요

우리 함께 세월은 잡을 수 없지만
마음 기대 따뜻하게 등 비비며
기우는 햇살 보내고
이글거린 아침노을 안으며
우리 청춘 무탈하게
살찌우며 지켜가요.

Love On Railway

We go on our way
Only both side by side.
And go over a far field
Putting arms around our shoulders.

Being far away, we lose interest in life,
Being near too, we can't go together.
So we grasp only our hands hard,
And both go on our way silently.

When the flower train passes, we both hold up it like a cloud,
When the heavy freight train passes, bearing up all our best,
We both work along day and night,
It's the steady railway, you and I love.

When the Petals fly up Together with fragrance
And the night soils scattet with tears wiped,
You and I, Going together in all seasons.
The lovable Railway.

- Tr. by Won Eung-Soon

Lee Jae-ho / Korea

*An Elder of Myungsung Presbyterian Church
*Member of the Literary Association of Gukbo, and of the Association of the Sijosarang in Korea
*Chairman of the United Society of Secondary School's Students in All Churches of Korea
*Counsellor for the Criminal Sufferers
*A Committee of the Criminal Mediation Commission
*Director of Planning, the Society of the World Poetry
*Address: Godeokrian Park 105-207, 152, Sangil-ro, Gangdong-gu, Seoul

기찻길 사랑

단 둘이 하나 되어
나란히 길을 간다
머나먼 들판을
어깨동무 길을 간다

멀어지면 살 수 없고
가까이도 갈 수 없어
단단히 손만 잡고
묵묵한 길을 간다

꽃열차 지나가면 구름처럼 떠받들고
무겁게 화차 가면 온몸으로 배기면서
주야장천 함께하는
그대와 나
변치 않는 철길

꽃잎이 날아오면 향기를 같이 내며
오물이 흩날리면 눈물을 함께 닦고
사시장철 함께 가는
그대와 나
사랑하는 기찻길

A Windy Day

There is a day that I desired to be a wind,
The wind blowing to me shaking the branches
Is a tonic more vitalizing than vitamin.

The gestures of the waving grasses,
The sound of the breaking boughs,
The wind blowing means
To make something exist,
The grass-field is to let fruits ripen,
The boughs are to make birds fly.

The wind, though it flutters at its own way,
Makes breasts and minds understand
To fill their empty parts,

There is a day I want to be a wind
Embracing it in my breast.

- Tr. by Won Eung-Soon

Lee Ji-young/Korea

*Hyosung University of French Literature,
*Member of Korean Society for Literature
*Member of International PEN Club in Korea Headquarters
*Member of Millennium Literature Society
*Vice President of the Association of Korea National Literature
*Vice President of the Society of Free Poets
*Received of the Korea National Literature Prize
*Received of the Literary Movement & Trend Literature Prize
*Books and Poetic Anthology : Running in grief and Want to wet like a moonlit' 'A diary on Wet day' 'A Dreaming Confidential Talk' 'The one who is easy of access and the one that discourages friendly advances' 'Holding a Mountain in one's arms" , A love of Snow Flower' and others.
*Address: Rm 1002, 311-Dong Donga Apt Dream Town, Pyeongchon-dong, Dongan-gu, Anyang-city, Gyeonggi-do, Korea

바람 부는 날

바람되 되고 싶은 날이 있다
나뭇가지를 흔들며 내게로 오는 바람은
비타민보다 생기를 주는 활력소

흔들리는 풀잎들의 손짓
부딪치는 나뭇가지들의 소리
바람이 분다는 건
무엇을 존재케 하는 뜻
풀밭은 열매를 익게 하고
나뭇가지는 새들을 날개 해

제멋대로 펄럭이는 바람이지만
빈 곳을 채워 주는
가슴과 가슴을 소통하게 해

항시 가슴에 품고 사는
바람이 되고 싶은 날이 있다

The Harvest Full Moon Day

For coming out to greet the rising moon as usual,
I, with Mr. Whang
Come up on the Yangwhajin bridge.

The Harvest Full Moon Day! When the brightly shining moon
Comes up to the ridge of the garden,
I have a great mind to see my mother's looks again.

My mother, sharing the clear mind with all town's people
And always opening the big gate, saying to them,
'We wish to be as good as the Harvest Full Day, not less, not more'.

To the son, the daughter-in-law, the grandsons
Who are working to plant the future in Bahrein, the hot country,
I earnestly pray for them to be a bright today and tomorrow
As big and round as the full moon.

- Tr. by Won Eung-Soon

Lee Sang-jin/Korea

*Born in 1941.
*Graduated from the Dept. of Law Korea Univ.
*Graduated from Graduate School,Kongguk Univ. (Ph.D.)
*Entered upon literary career through the monthly magazine "Literary Movement & Trend"
*Served the Governor of the World Poetry Research Institute.
*Serves concurrently as professor of a school of law at Dongguk University.
*Poetic Anthology : "A Water Well of Home(2006)" "A Way(2011)"

*Address: zip cord 04005, 1-gil, 16, no. 201, City-villa of Ganbyeon, Dongkyo-ro, Mapo-Gu, Seoul, Korea

대보름

여느 때와 같이 떠오르는 보름달을
마중 나가기 위해 황형(黃兄)과 함께
양화진 다리 위에 오른다.

한가위! 휘영청 밝은 달이 어렴풋이
동산 마루에 떠오르면,
또다시 어머님의 모습이 새로워진다.

더도 덜도 말고 한가위만 같아라 하시며
항상 대문을 열어 놓고 온 동네에
정갈한 마음을 나누어 주시던 어머님

열사(熱砂)의 나라, 바레인에서
미래를 심고 있는 아들, 며느리, 손자들
보름달처럼 크고 둥굴게
밝은 오늘과 내일이 되길 기원한다.

A Good Friend at Meeting
- Soju

The moment I saw you first,
How was I thread and afraid?

So I didn't like you,
Even though I had to confront you,
I was forced to kiss you
Without giving my heart.

One day
When I was tired out and hard in life,
I suddenly seek for you.

You
Fondled me my mind,

Lim Byeong-jeon/Korea

*Born at Gochang, Jeon Buk, Korea
*Made a new debut a Poet from the Gigumunhak
*Member of the Korean Writers' Association
*Member of the Poetry and Arts Association of Korea
*Director of the Writers Association of the Gigumunhak
*Secretary General of the Mapo Writers' Association
*Executive Member of O-Weol-Ae
*Poetic Anthology: The Stairs of the Paradese, etc.
*Won the Main Prize of the "Heo-nan-sul-han"(the 27th)
*E-mail : limbyungjeon@hanmail.net
*Address: zip cord(03941) 230, World cup buk-ro, Mapo-gu, Seoul, Korea.

Stimulating a courage
To acquire affection for you.

Now
When I meet you,
To kiss with you is always happy,
Even I like your fragrance.

We are good friends
Being along with delight and sadness
When we meet each other.

- Tr. by Won Eung-Soon

만나면 좋은 친구
–소주

너를 처음 본 순간
얼마나 두렵고 무서웠던가

그래서 너를 좋아하지 못했고
어쩔 수 없이 너와 마주쳐도
내 마음 주지 못하고
마지못해 입맞춤 했었지

어느 날
삶에 지치고 힘들 때
문득 너를 찾았지

너는
내 마음 달래 주었고
용기를 주었고
점점 정이 들었지

지금은
너를 만나면
입맞춤이 즐겁고
너의 향기를 좋아한다

우리는 기쁨도
슬픔도 같이하는
만나면 좋은 친구

One Hundred Years, Solitude of Being and Extinction

We thought highly of life
With reverence for the alive beings.
The days that they held humankind in their bosom
Are changed into the lonely love of one hundred years now.
Raven(갈까마귀?) with no resistant gesture
Follows after signals of wind,
And he flies coloring blue sky as black color
Attached in addition with his black wing's brushes.
His eyes, lost past's will
As the untied eulalias on the hillside
Are looking back between their white scattered threads

Maeng Sook-young/Korea

*Graduated from Dept. of English Lit. of Sungkyunkwan Univ. Seoul
*Graduated from the Graduate School of Han Sei Univ,(M.A. Degree)
*Taught at High School as an English Teacher
*Director of Seoul Branch in the Korean Writers' Association
*Director of the Contemporary Poets' Association of Korea
*Chief Editor, the Society of the World Poetry
*Director of the Christian Literary Authors' Association of Korea
*Won a great Prize of Changjo Literature of Korea
*Won a Prize of the Yanchun Literature
*Poetical Anthology: *The Light Shining with Love
*The Dreaming Wings
*Address : 299 Omok-ro, yangcheon-gu, Mokdong Trapalis Western Avenue, A-2002
*E-mail: maeng1215@hanmail.net

Flapping in the wind.
He pines for the day not to come back again,
And looks a beautiful world
Over the frosted gaze,
Gazing it afar unfamiliarly.

- Tr. by Won Eung-Soon

백년, 그 존재와 소멸의 고독

살아있는 것에의 경외감으로
생명을 존귀히 여겼네
인류를 품에 안고 가던 날들은
이제 백년의 고독한 사랑이 되어 버렸네
갈까마귀 거부할 수 없는 몸짓으로
바람의 손짓 따라가네
검은 날개붓으로 푸른 하늘 까맣게
덧칠하며 날아가네
지난날의 의지를 잃어버린
언덕 위 억새풀 풀어진 시선
하얗게 흐트러진 갈기 끝으로
바람을 날리며 뒤돌아보네
다시 못 올 그날을 그리워하네
성에 낀 시야 너머로
아름다운 세상을 바라보네
낯설게 멀리 바라보네

A Lettuce Wrapped Rice

One wicker basket of lettuce and crown daisy
That a farmer farmed himself was given to me.
When a spoonful of rice
In soybean paste forming as one wrapped rice
Was put in my mouth,
An old friend with stooped shoulders
And black dirt under his nails,
Takes his seat silently
In a corner of his mind.
Mixing together friendship like old pickles
Being wet with sweat,
I put one wrapped rice
In my mouth again.

- Tr. by Won Eung-Soon

Nam Chang-hee/ Korea

*Pen Name: Inseok
*Born in July 14, 1945
*Graduated from Suwon High School
*Graduated from Chung-ang University
*General Manager of Los Angeles Agency of Korea First Bank
*Won the Prize as a new Poet at the Christian Literature of Korea
*Prof, of National Far Eastern Univ. of Russia
*Founder and Chairman of GiL Primary School of Pakistan
*Director, the Society of the World Poetry
*Address: (13532) Apt. 606-801, Pangyoyeok-Ro 100, Bundang-gu Seongnam City.

쌈

친구가 농사지었다고
상추 쑥갓 한 소쿠리를 주었다
밥 한 숟갈에
강된장 올려
한 쌈
입에 넣으니
구부정한 어깨
손톱 밑이 까맸던
늙다리 친구
마음 한 구석에 슬며시
들어와 앉는다
땀방울로 녹여 낸
묵은지 닮은 우정
섞어 버무려
또 한 쌈
입에 넣는다

It's Good To Keep Long

Recollection
Keeps long,
That should be savory as scorched rice.

The first love
Remains long,
When it is as pretty as a little fingernail
Tinted well with a peach-colored.

The first affection
Keeps long more,
When it is such a bosom
As Indian corn slightly exposed
Like a soysauce-bowl.

Oh Hui-chang/ Korea

*Born at Noho -ri, Bugang-myeon, Sejong City, Korea
*Pen name: Samhodang
*Director of the Ministry of Justice
*Administrator of Rectifying Office in Daejeon City
*Essayist(from the Essay Literature 1997)
*Poet(from the quarterly magazine "the Munyesajo, 1998)"
*Committee of the Literary Exchange between North and South in the Literary Association of Korea, and of the Korean Headquarter, International PEN Club (A Corporation)
*Literary Works:
Essay Anthology: "Come after Praying for offspring", etc. 5 Vols.
Poetical Anthology: "A Blossom of Flame". etc. 7 Vols.
*Address: 130 Mokdong-ro, Yangcheon-gu, Mokdong Apt. 1402 dong No202, Seoul, Korea
*E-mail: samhodang@hanamil.net/ Tel: 010-6353-3535

Yearning
Remains long,
When we strike our heart
Unable to tolerate any more.

Flavor of soysauce also
As it gets old is good,
If my destiny(karma) and friendship
Also are joined on ever and ever,
If would be better.

- Tr. by Won Eung-Soon

오래 되어야 좋다

추억은
누룽지처럼 구수해야
오래 남는다

첫사랑은
봉숭아 물 곱게 들인
새끼손톱처럼 이뻐야
오래 남는다

첫 정은
살~작 드러난
옥수수 같은 앞니
간장종지 같은 젖가슴이래야
더욱 오래 남는다

그리움은
더는 못 참는다고
가슴을 두들겨 패야
오래 남는다

장맛도
오래 된 것이 좋듯
나의 인연도 우정도
오래 오래 이어지면
좋겠다

Dokdo Ile, Our Land

The place where our minds are put in
Together with our love and concerns,
Is called Dokdo Ile.

Dokdo Ile melts our frozen bosom in the warm words,
And soothes our joys and sorrows with casting our eyes on it,
So it is called Dokdo Ile.

Dokdo Ile, being away from us,
Only with our support and yearning,

Oh Jin-hwan/Korea

*Born in Suanbo in Chung-ju
*Graduated from Han-yang Univ., Dept. of Eng
*Graduated from the Dep of business administration of Yeon-se University * Member of Korean Writer's Association
*Member of the International Association of Writers in Korea Headquarters
*Vice secretary general of the World Poetry Research Institute
*President, the Society of the World Poetry
*President of Seocho Writers' Association
*President of literary association 'An Annual Ring'
*Won The 27th World Poetry Gaya Golden Crown Prize
*Won The 12nd Seocho Literature Prize
*Awarded the prize of the monthly magazine 'Literature 21'
*Awarded the prize of Tam-mee literature
*Awarded the prize of cultural exchange between India and Korea
*Awarded the Medal of Nokjoguenjeong
*Poetical Anthology : "A Persimmon left for Magpie" "In the bosom of you after becoming A Crane" "The Mountain Doesn't Lay Blame on Clouds" etc.
*Literary Works: A commemorative work 'A fisherman who puts a bait for a man.
*Address: Zip Code 03633, #34gil 46, Tongil-ro, Inwangsan Hyundae Apt, 109-902, Seodaemun-gu, Seoul Korea.
*Hand phone : 010-2324-3454 *E-mail : oh3454@korea, com

Is our companion and friend.

As far as you exist with us,
Dokdo Ile is a lovable being we can cry and laugh together
By inseparably bound up with the sweet and noble friendship.

Dokdo Ile is a pride and hope of Korea,
Standing aloft gracefully between high waves of the wild sea.
As our reliable watchman.

It is a mysterious Island,
A great pleasure of our race and a treasure,
Ah, a boastful Dokdo Ile!

- Tr. by Won Eung-Soon

우리의 땅 독도

가슴이 담아져 있는 곳
사랑하는 마음에 담아
걱정해주는 독도입니다

따뜻한 말로 얼어붙은 가슴을 녹이고
늘 바라보는 그 눈빛이
애환을 달래주는 독도입니다

멀리 있어도 마음으로 의지하고
그리워하는 것만으로도
우리의 동반자 우리의 친구인 독도입니다

너가 존재하는 한 같이 아파하고
함께 웃을 수 있는 나라를 지켜주는
지란지교 같은 독도입니다

출렁이는 바다, 우둑 솟은 자연의 우아함
마음 든든한 겨레의 파수꾼
대한민국의 자랑이며 희망을 주는 독도입니다

신비의 섬,
겨레의 기쁨이고 보배입니다
아! 자랑스러운 독도

A Peony Flower

July is crossing the threshold,
And now summer season is getting ripen more and more.

The peony flower with graceful peony flower
In the deep valley filled with dark green color,

Here is a woman, the Chosun's traditional one
With a round chignon combed out, in claret colored coat string,
A white silk apron and jacket.

You, you are so beautiful and so fragrant,
That I stroke your head stopping my way on.

As woman, how pretty you are!
I see you've a clear and noble breathing,
And hear your clear voice of quietness(stillness).

Oh Suk-hyeon/ Korea

*First Debut as a new Poet from "the Simsang Literature"
*Member of the Korea Headquarter, International PEN Club
*Vice Director of the Commission for Cultivation of our Language, the Korea Literary Man's Association
*Member of the Seocho Branch Association of Literature
*Director of the Literary Society of the World Poetry
*Vice President of "the National Arts and Culture of Liberty and the President of the Seoul Branch
*Prizes: Won the Second Prize of the Literary Writing Contest of So-Wol

How can it be so and so pretty!

Also your so strong character as our tenderness,
In which has warmness and pungency,
Is emitting around the mountain.

- Tr. by Won Eung-Soon

산 목련화(함박꽃)

유월이 문지방을 넘는다
여름이 점점 익어갈 무렵

초록 흠뻑 젖은 산골짜기
기품 있는 모습 산 목련화

참빗질 쪽 찐 머리, 자주 고름
하얀 명주 치마저고리 입은
조선의 여인 여기 있구나

너, 하도 곱고 향기로워
잠시 발길 멈춰 쓰다듬어본다.

어찌 그리 고울까 여인아!
청아하고 고결한 숨결을 본다.
고요의 맑은 물소리가 들린다.

어쩜, 그렇게도 그렇게도

또한
속내는, 따뜻하고 맵기도 한
여린 듯 강한 품격이 산내로 퍼진다.

A Sky of my Hometown

Mt. Duryun Ranges linking Gangjin and Haenam,
The sonorous fragrance in the dense camellia forest,
The white clouds floating from a place far far away
And twilight of the evening burning in the violet sky,
Are those of my childhood coming across when I closed my eyes.

A summer day when I came over 'Woosul Summit',
When We(brother and sister), who had been to our mother's maiden home,
Were resting and soaking feet in water at the large lake,
The groups of fishes played on the sky and clouds reflected under water,
The water sound from the Mandeoksa Fall was heard.

Park Hoe-sang/ Korea

*Greaduated from Dept. of English Literature of Seokang University.
*Served as a English Teacher, Organizing the Drama Class and the English Newspaper, and Retired as a Vice-Principle.
*President's Reward, and the Order of National Service Merit.
*A Life Member of Academy of Philosophy.
*Director, the Society of the World Poetry
*Director of the Society of the Korea Mental Science.
* Vice President of Writer's Society at the Munhakshinmun.
* A Committee of the Reward and Punishment at the Korean Writers' Association.
* Address: [03038] 29-9, 5 Nagil, Pilwoondae-Ro, Parkgoldville no. 601, Jonro-Gu, Seoul, Korea.

The air was shimmering from the budding field and mountain,
The sunlight falling down on the swaying grass leaves,
The sound of dead leaves trembling in the cold wind,
And the white snowflakes fell endlessly,
The silkworm without tears had not its rainbow, has it?

At the night when the tired people in a strange land didn't sleep,
Listen to my sad story,
Not other men's one always from a telephone
Crying, laughing, talking in my sleep, murmuring nonsense,
The young people live in aspiration, and the old live in retrospection.

- Tr. by Won Eung-Soon

고향 하늘

강진 해남을 잇는 두륜산 줄기
울창한 동백 숲 은은한 향기
천리 밖을 떠도는 흰 구름
보랏빛 하늘에 타는 저녁노을
눈감으면 떠오르는 유년의 고향산천

우슬재 넘어오던 어느 여름날
외갓집 다녀오던 우리 남매가
커다란 호숫가에 발 담그고 쉴 때
물밑 하늘 구름 위로 노닐던 고기떼
만덕사 폭포 그 물소리 들려오네

움트는 산과 들에 아지랑이 오르고
하늘대는 풀잎에 내리는 햇살
찬바람에 떨고 있는 가랑잎 소리
한 없이 내리는 하얀 눈송이
눈물 없는 누에는 무지개가 없다던가

타향살이 지친 몸 잠 못 드는 밤
어디론가 뉘에겐가 전화기 들고
네 서러움 제쳐두고 내 설움 들어봐라
울다가 웃다가 잠꼬대냐 넋두리냐
청춘은 희망에 살고 노년은 추억에 산다

The Waiting Ache

The itinerary journey of waiting
Always makes us ache our minds,

We expect a pleasure
With a throbbing of dawn.

The mind to endure the cold frost facing it directly,
Learns endurance,

Grieving the pain of love
Whether to get connected or not,

Moving off one step aside,
I knock the window.

- Tr. by Won Eung-Soon

Park Jong-hwa/Korea

*Graduated from Dept. of Industrial Engineering of the Graduate School, Kyung Hee Univ. (M.A. Degree)
*Director of the Korea Research for Poisoning Psychological Counselling
*Secretary General of the World Literature Association of Environment
*Prof. of the Healing Center of the Korea Prevention for Poisoning
*Received a Great Prize of the World Environment Literature
*Poetical Works: "Retrospection Flows as a Poem", "At a Junction of Life", etc.
*English Poetical Works: "A Mother's Love", "Brilliant Life"

기다림의 아픔

기다림의 여정은
늘 가슴 아프게 하고

새벽의 설레임으로
기쁨을 기다리네

찬 서리 맞으며 견뎌내는 마음은
인내를 배우고

사랑의 아픔 이어질까
가슴조이며

한 발짝 물러서서
창문을 두드려 보네

The Way 2

Today
Also my shape is sad
For what greed am I wondering about
Between the forked path?

Today
After roaming about a long while,
I take a rest a little while
Under an aged tree.

Though the aged tree for its own life
Always has been beautiful in the place,
My footmarks, being rubbed down at heel
Are poor in the forked lane.

Park Youn-ki/Korea

*Pen Name: Chosan.
*Born in Andong, Gyeongbuk, Korea
*Graduated from Pacheon Primary School and Cheonsong High School.
*Retired at SDI of Samsung(1999)
*First Debut as a Poet through "Literary Movement & Trend"
*Recorded as a Poet in "The Encyclopedia of Korean Poetry"
*A Member of the Association of Literary Movement & Trend.
*Director of the Society of the World Poetry.
*Poetic Anthology : "the Twilight of Nakdong River"
*Won the Main Prize of the 31st the Society of the World Poetry
*E-mail : buna2000@hanmail.net
*Address: 15-3, Chosan 2-gil, Habuk-myeon, Yangsan-si, Gyeongsangnam-do, Korea

Covetously
A half of my life
Has been roamed about in the forked lane.

Being tired of roaming about,
Today also
Is a sad day.

- Tr. by Won Eung-Soon

길 2

오늘도
내 모습이 슬프다
무슨 욕심으로 헤매고 있을까
갈림길에서,

오늘도
한참이나 헤매다가
고목나무 밑에서 잠시
쉬어 본다.

고목은 한세월
제자리에서 늘 아름다운데
뒤축 닳은 내 발자국은
갈림길에서 불쌍하다.

욕심스럽게도
내 인생의 절반은
갈림길에서 헤맸다.

헤매다가 지친
오늘도
슬픈 하루.

A Landscape of Cheongsan Island

Cheongsan Island where the green barley is spread out greenly,
As if the sea is rocking on the winds,
The green waves surge.

An old wayfarer, visited the island to forget the busting city life,
Is walking slowly on the path of its stonewall.
This beauty moving slowly that a "yellow dog" and a farmer
Carrying A-form on his back fades away slowly
Turning around its stonewall,
Makes late afternoon be leisured more.

Park Young-yul/Korea

*Born at Yanggu, Gangwon-do, Korea
*Graduated from Graduate School of Jungang Univ.
*Graduated from California Univ. with Ed. Degree
*Served as a Prof, of Seokyeong Univ. and its Chief of a Pastor, and Vice-president of Jungang Theological Graduate University
*A Standing Director of General Alliance of the Korean Christianity
*A Vice-President of the Association of the Christian Literature of Korea
*A Member of the Korean Writers' Association
*Director, the Society of the World Poetry
*A Member of the International PEN in the Korea Pen Headquarter
*A Director of the Modern Poets' Association of Korea
*A Chairman of the Mapo Writers' Society
*Won the Prize of Literature form the Monthly magazine "The Korean Poetry"(1990)
*Collection of Poems: "As a Stream of a Wind" *Writing Books: "The Leadership and the Church Growth", "The Only Hour of the Jesus and I", and lots of Dissertations, etc.
Address : Changjeon-Ro 2Gil, 27(No. 103)
*E-mail: holyhill091@hanmai.net
*Tel. 02-717-4536 H.P: 010-5253-7932

That the brood hen runs about anxiously
On the way of a stonewall
And a spaniel and a doggie also toddle about here and there,
Looks very warm hearted.

An old wayfarer, visiting to rest from his city life,
Walks softly on the lane of its stonewall at sunset,
As if some people in "p'ansori named Seopeonjae"
Walked slowly together on the country path
Dancing and singing along to the drums
Emanating their grudges.

The wayfarer in the Oriental Drawing also is leisured.

- Tr. by Won Eung-Soon

청산도 풍경

청보리가 시퍼렇게 펼쳐진 청산도
바다가 바람에 일렁일렁 거리듯
초록의 물결이 보리밭에 출렁거린다

도시의 빠른 분주함을 잊고자 찾은
청산도 돌담길을 느릿느릿 걷는다
누렁이가 지게 진 농부와
돌담길을 돌아 천천히 사라지는
느림의 미학이 고즈넉한 늦은 오후가
더욱 한가롭다

구불구불 이어진 돌담길을
씨암탉이 뒤뚱뒤뚱 거리고
발발이 멍멍이가 졸랑졸랑대며
걷는 것이 정겹다

분주하게만 살아온 삶이
한숨 쉬어 가고자 찾은 노년의 나그네가
그 옛날 서편제 노랫가락이
북 장단에 덩실덩실 춤추며 한을 쏟아내던
그 길을 뉘엿뉘엿 스러지는 석양에
돌담길을 걷는다

동양화 속 나그네도 한가롭다

The Passing of Time

No matter how much you try to
hold,
Only a bucket of sea watter left.
One day Left when you leave
empty-handed.
Only a handful of dirt from the hills,

Dreams cry out loud
Under the pouring rain,
Emptiness lingers
Behind the trail of the wind

Seo Keun-hee/ Korea

*Born at Hamyang, Kyungnam, Korea
*Graduated from Dept. of the Dietetics of Food at Sook Myung Woman's Univ.
*Member of the Korean Writers' Association of Literature
*Member of the Korea Headquarter, International PEN
*Member of the Woman Literary Writers of Korea
Prizes: Won the New Poet's Prize from "the Space of Literature)" (1989), Won the New Poet's Prize from "the Modern Poets' Association of Korea"(2018), Won the Prize of "Hernanseolheon"(2000), Won the great Prize of Literature "the Lim Young-chang"(2018), Won the Prize of Poetic Part of Literature for the !00th National Foundation of Korea (2019)
*Poetical Anthology: "A Scroll of Time", "Gathering Up Sunbeams", "The Sunbeam's Stagnation", "Fill with the Sunbeams 1, 2"
The Coterie Anthology: "The Poetic Society of the 7th Day"
*Address: 17 Jungang Park Street, Bundang-Gu, Hanyang Apt. 325dong 401, Sungnam City, Geonggi-do, Korea(Seohyeon-dong Sibeom Apt.)

Love is just a gesture.
How much more has to be
drained
To once again be a flower in
a bloom,
To be a butterfly wings free of
sorrow,
In that place high up where the
Sun shines on.

세월

아무리 움켜 쥐어 봐도
한 쪽박으로 뜬 바닷물
어느날 빈 손으로 떠나면
산허리 허무는 흙 한 줌

내리는 비 한 줄기에
꿈은 젖어 울고
허전한 바람의 뒷자락
사랑은 손짓일 뿐
얼마나 더 비우고 비워야
햇살 익어가는 저 높은 곳에서
다시 필 꽃이 될까
시름 접은 날개의 나비 될까.

Like the Grass Leaf of that Field

When we hang around at a forked road
Not knowing to choose which way,
I desired to meet a man like a tree
Who buried a water pail deeply into the ground,
To give warmth for the frozen feet.

If life is a process seeking for love,
Even trampling under foot, like the sprouting grass's seeds,
Hanging a smart mind above the sky
For a moment with folding it,
I shall embrace hot another I
Being called out in me.

Shin Dong-myeong/Korea

*Born in Seoul
*Started a literary career through the magazine 'Literary Movement & Trend'(essay)
*Started a literary career through the magazine 'Literary 21'
*Member of the international PEN in Korea Headquarters
*Member of Korean Woman Writer's Association
*Vice President, the Society of the World Poetry
*Member of Modern poetry association
*Member of Korean essayist Association
*Won the Kaya Gold Crown of the World Poetry, etc
*Published poetical works: The Will of Wings'. A Short and Long Story.
*Published literary jottlings: From Han River to Senue
*Stray notes: A Watercolor Painting in the Picture
*Address: 502, Hyundae Apt, 171-61, Bulgwang2-dong, Eunpyong-gu, Seoul, Korea
*E-mail: sdm1445@hanmail.net

Yes, this man, don't say we are lonely now!

Whoever can take down
The heavy burden(life itself) easily
That we pack on the back or take it down?
Even the leaves of grass unknown in the field
Are so shaking and rising with their burdens saddled.

- Tr. by Won Eung-Soon

저 들판의 풀잎처럼

갈림길 이르러 갈 곳 몰라
서성일 때
땅 속 깊숙이 물관부 묻은
나무 같은 사람을 만나고 싶다
언 발 내밀면 따스한 온기 보태 줄

삶이 사랑 찾아가는 여정이라면
짓밟혀도 다시 움터 오는 풀싹처럼
아린 마음 잠시 접어
하늘에 걸어 놓고
내 안의
또 다른 나 불러내 뜨겁게 포옹하리

그래, 이 사람아 이젠 외롭다고 하지 말자

등짐지기도 내려놓기에도 벅찬 삶
누군들 무겁다고
쉬이 벗어 놓을 수 있겠나
들판의 이름 모를 풀잎조차 저렇듯
제 생을 업고 흔들리며 일어서는데.

Mother's Apron

Mother!
I called her name silently,
But my heart moves about uneasy.
She fostered her six children with pleasure,
And she takes under her neighbors under her broad and pretty apron,
Always blooming a laugh-flower around the dining table,
So this place is like a flower garden to mother,

Saying, 'good, all right'.

Shin Young-ok/Korea

*Pen Name: Hyesan. *Born at Goesan in Cheongju, Korea.
*Graduated from Cheongju Teachers' School, from a College of Education and served many years at Schools.
*First Debut as a Poet by the Recommandation of the poet, Kim Kyeong-lin, Jeon Kyu-tae, through the quarterly Magazine <Literature and Consciousness>.
*Director, the Society of the World Poetry
*Activities: Member of the Kore Writers' Association &its Steering Committee; of the International PEN: of the Christian Writers' Association of Korea; of the Modern Poets' Association of Korea; of the Female Writers' Association of Korea, etc.
*A Collection of Poems: 1) The Sound Calling Me Today 2) The Traces as the Smell of Soil 3) The River Deepened of Itself 4) Falling in the Mountain's Light(Translated Korean into English), etc
*Receiving Awards: *Won a Prize of Heo-nan-seol-hern's Literature; of Young-rang's Literature; of the Children's Literature; of the Korea Race Writer's; And Received the Order of National Service Merit 'Dongback-Jang'.
*Recorded in Time Capsule as a Writer for a Centennial Christianity of Korea.
*E-mail: yoshin39@hanmail.net
*HP: 010-7368-3622

Now the empty place of Mother,
Informing all of us that, with her rough hands and loin,
'Mothers in the world have done to us like that,
And so even the big or small worm and animals'
Is felt to be big to us.

Today
Holding the mother's warm apron,
I want to embrace the mother in my breast.
Mother, who ia always alive in me,
Enjoy glory with God
And have rest peacefully in an eternal paradise.

- Tr. by Won Eung-Soon

어머니의 앞치마

어머니.
가만히 불러만 봐도 가슴이 설렙니다.
우리 칠남매 기쁨으로 기르시고
이웃까지 감싸 안던 넓고 고운 치맛자락
밥상머리에 피어나던 웃음꽃
당신은 언제나 '됐다. 괜찮다.' 하시며
사계절 가꿔 오신 꽃밭입니다

거칠어지던 손길 아픈 허리
'세상 어미들은 다 그렇단다.
크고 작은 짐승 벌레까지'
들려주시던 말씀들
날이 갈수록 커져가는 어머니의 빈자리

오늘은
포근한 어머니 치맛자락 휘감고
내 품에 꼭 안아드리고 싶습니다.
내 안에 늘 살아계신 어머니
영원한 낙원 그 나라에서
영광을 받으소서. 평안을 누리소서

Mist Flower of the Sea at Dawn

The sea tumbles yearning for land,
I loss about longing for the sea,
The dragon belch of betrayal,
Water denying being Water.
The sea bounces like al steel spring.

When the sounds of waves glitter white
As mist flowers,
I lie there as a sea anemone
Dreaming of revolution,
There where the beetle shells have built a net
on the asphalt.
I`ll return, I`ll return there,
Escorting the aimless days like the pisces
To the primordial sea trench.

Sohn Hea-il/ Korea

*President of the Korea Pen Headquarter of International PEN
*Debut:First Debut as a Poet from monthly Magazine of ≪the Simunhak≫, in 1978.
*Works: Peetical Works : 「Wangin's Moon」, 「A Mobile Real Estate Agent 'Trutabang' and Magpie's Nest」, and 「New Jasaneobo」
*Award: The Literary Prize of Seoul National Univ./ the Literary Prize of the Simunhak/ of the Honik/ The Preze of the Seocho Literature/ the Prize of the Sowol Literature, etc.

As we drink the middle age
In a tavern the some seashore,
The heart-affected waves are sliced as raw fish dish.
The mist flower of the sea at daybreak
Bloom in the bell sound ringing blue with flashes.

- Trans, Ko Chang-soo

새벽바다 안개꽃

바다는 육지가 그리워 출렁이고
나는 바다가 그리워 뒤척인다
물이면서 물이기를 거부하는
모반의 용틀임
용수철로 튀는 바다

물결소리 희디희게
안개꽃으로 빛날 때
아스팔트에 둥지 튼 갑충(甲蟲)의 깍지들
나도 그 속에 말미잘로 누워
혁명을 꿈꾼다.
돌아가리라, 돌아가리라.
덧없는 날들을 어족처럼 데불고
시원(始原)의 해구(海構)로

우리가 어느 바닷가 선술집에서
불혹을 마시고 있을 때
더위 먹은 파도는 생선회로 저며지고
섬광 푸른 종소리에 피는
새벽바다 안개꽃

I Ask Stars

I ask stars
In the silent night.

About when shall the full moon
Above the garden?

Whispering by themselves
The stars don't answer,

They let me tell
The story waiting the full moon.

Wee Maeng-ryang/ Korea

*Pen-name: Sihern *Date of Birth: April 18, 1940
*Born at Bangchon-ri, Kwansan-eup, Jangheung-kun, Jeonnam, Korea
*Graduated from a College of Agriculture in Korea Univ.
*First Debut as a new Poet from the Monthly Magazine "Korea Poetry"
*Debuted as an Essayist from "the Media of Literature"
*Member of the Korean Writers' Association, *of the Modern Poets' Association of Korea, *of the International Pen in Quarters of the Korean PEN, *of the Korea Literary Society for Reciting and Performance, *of the Christian Writers' Association of Korea, *of the Christian Poets' Association of Korea, *of the Literary Society of the World Poetry of Korea
*Director, the Society of the World Poetry
*Vice-President of the Mapo Writers' Association
*A Representative of 'Willy Trading Co.'(Present)
*Literary Works: A Lonely Lane(Poems and Essays), The Far Future(Collection of Poems), Hoesungsaego(Joint Author), Jeonghern's Posthumous Works, etc
*Address: Postal Number 04526, #29-1, Namdaemun-ro, Jung-gu, Seoul City
*E-mail: agentewilly@hotmail.com
* H.P.: 010-8939-2620

One couple of rabbits under the cinnamon tree,
Beating medical plants for the long life in a mortar,

They said to me
That they would give a pack of herbs.

- Tr. by Won Eung-Soon

별들에게 묻노라

고요한 밤하늘
별들에게 묻노라

동산 위에 보름달은
언제쯤 떠오를까

별들은 대답 않고
저희끼리 속삭이더니

보름달 기다리는
사연을 말하라네

계수나무 아래 토끼 한 쌍
불로장생 약방아 찧어

나에게도 한 첩
준다고 했지요.

A Prayer in Autumn

The crickets and all kinds of the grass insects
Are sitting up all night prayer over night,
You brought a bright dawn to us.
Let us love this scarlet dawn
Beginning to awake one day.

Under the scorching sunshine
You, hearing an ardent wish of the scarecrow
Who takes trouble all day,
Gave rich autumn.
Let us love the black field which finished the harvesting.

When the white sea gulls dance in groups
On the blue sea,
The white clouds in the high and blue sky

Yang Hae-gwan/ Korea

*Pen Name: Shinsan
*Born in Youngam-gun, Jeonnam, Korea
*Member of the Garden of Lit.
*Member of the Mapo Writers' Association
*Member of the World Poetry Society
*Joint Literary Work: I Want to Go to Temporary Station
*Poetic Anthology: A Song of Mt. Baekdusan
*Job: A Licensed Real State Agent at Mapo Office
*Address : 48, World Cup buk-ro 38-gil, Mapo-gu, Seoul, Korea
*E-mail : ssbd 5111@hanmail.net

Flow with a west wind.
Lord, let us love the peaceful white clouds.

The things, filled plentifully, are emptied soon,
The place, emptied, will be filled up soon,
To empty and to fill up are God's providence,
Let us thank and love one by one
To put the finishing touches on deepening autumn.

- Tr. by Won Eung-Soon

가을 속의 기도

귀뚜라미와 온갖 풀벌레들이
밤을 새워 철야기도를 하니
당신은 밝은 새벽을 보내 주셨습니다
하루가 막 깨어나는
이 도홍빛 새벽을 사랑하게 하소서

뙤약볕 아래에서
온종일 수고하는 허수아비의
간절한 염원을 들으시고
당신은 풍요의 가을을 주셨습니다
추수 끝난 검은 들판을 사랑하게 하소서

푸른 바다 위에
하얀 갈매기가 군무를 추면
높고 푸른 하늘가에
흰 구름이 갈바람 따라 흘러갑니다
주여 평화로운 흰 구름을 사랑하게 하소서

풍요하게 채워진 것들은 곧 비워지고
비어 있던 곳은 가득 채워지리니
비움과 채움이 당신의 섭리인즉
깊어가는 가을을 갈무리하는 것들을
낱낱이 감사하며 사랑하게 하소서

The Path Going to You

When a forest is careless
The path is in sight.
On my sad path in the yellow soil colored
For a home town,

A warbler cries
So as for my finger tips to tremble.
When a dazzling sky of my hometown
Enters your mind,
The wood is careless

Yoon Hyoung-soon / Korea

*Born at Daegu-myun, Kangjin-gun, Jeon-Nam, Korea
*Graduated from College of Agriculture, Jeon-Nam University
Served at Ministry office of Agriculture for 20 Years, and at National Agrecultural Co-operation Federation for 13 Years
*Manager of the Kindred Society of the Haenam Family "Yun"
*Received the Prize in Literary Contest for Poetry under the Auspices of Jeonnam Daily Newspaer(1965)
*Member of the World Poetry Institute
* Address : #89 Jeongpyung-Ro, Hyundae Prime Apt. 207-501, Suji-Gu, Youngin City, Gyeonggi-Do, Korea
* Mobile : 010-9583-5003

The path going to you
Comes in sight.

The wood is to be careless
For you to be visible.

- Tr. by Won Eung-Soon

너에게 가는 길

숲이 무심할 때
길이 보이더라
황톳빛 서러운
고향 길에서

살끝이 시리도록
꾀꼬리 울더라
눈시린
고향 하늘이
가슴에 와 있을 때
숲은 무심하고
너에게 가는 길이 보이더라

숲이 무심해야
네가 보이더라.

The Cayenne Peppers

On one summer's day
With the warmest heat of the sun,
I went to my old home.

The cayenne peppers of the field
That the single mother
Reclaimed nicely
At her yard under the hot sunshines,
Were hung in clusters,
So the red pepper's leaves
Was suspended lowly.

In a metal bucket filled with water fully,
I sprinkled the dry earth pouring it,
Soon their leaves seemed to be animated.

Yun Ja/ Korea

*Born at Suncheon, Jeonnam, Korea
*Graduated from Dept. of Social Welfare, Suncheon First Univ., Jeonnam, Korea
*Won the great Prize of the Public Subscription, March, A Literary Writing Contest of the Korea Dasun Artist's Association, Korea
*Won the Prize for a new Poet from the Poetry Part, the Dasun Literature
*Member of the Society of the World Poetry
*Member of the Dasun Literary Writer's Association of Korea
*Poetical Anthology: "Writing Poem as Scattering Flower Seeds"
*Address: #3gil 8, Sung-dong, Jungang Hights no. 904 Suncheon City, Jeonnam, Korea
*Mobile : 010-8980-6848

Toward sundown slowly,
Hastening to me, 'It gets dark, go quick.'
She followed me up to the gate.

Other cayenne pepper trees
Holding their hands highly like such,
Said to me, 'Yunja, don't go.'

At the moment, as if the dry hot cayenne pepper's smell
Goes past by me, my nose tip was smarting and wrinkling.

- Tr. by Won Eung-Soon

그 여름날 고추

태양의 열기로
푹푹 찌는 여름
친정집 갔었지

홀로 계신 어머니께서
알뜰하게 일궈 놓으신
마당가 고추밭
뜨거운 뙤약볕 아래
고추 주렁주렁 열려 있고
고추나무 잎사귀
축 늘어져 있었네

양동이 물 가득 채워
메마른 흙에 붓고 뿌려 주니
금세 생기 도는 듯했지

뉘엿뉘엿 해 질 녘
캄캄해진다 어서 가거라 재촉하시고
문밖까지 따라오시며 그러셨지

여그 고추나무들이
양팔을 요렇게 벌리고
윤자야 가지 마라 그란다

그 순간 마른 고추 매운 냄새 스치듯
코끝이 아리고 찡해졌었지.

The Burning Sun*

The sun burns,
It was suffocated as our earth should be melted down
By a scorching heat of last summer,
How much it was so hot,
Does it swallow up even the sun?

The burning sun is not a subject
Of the moving picture of the action adventure in Hollywood.

It's the place where our male power of Gangnam in higher classes
And the organized violence are swinging their arms.

We name the sadistic symptoms 'the Burning Sun'
Resulting by the burning desire of youth.

- Tr. by Won Eung-Soon

*Burning Sun: It's the name of the wineshop, a kind of cafe' at Gangnam.

Yun Su-a / Korea

*Born at Chon-An, Chung-Nam, Korea.
*A Reciter of Poetry
*Recommended as an essayist winning the prize
*Director of General, the Society of the World Poetry
*Editorial staff of magazine Jigumunhak('98~'01)
*Vice President of Guro Literary Association.
*President of 'Siwoollim Poet's Coterie.
*Collection of Poems : Festival of Volcano, Poem, How much do I pay?
*Address : 104-405, Hyundae HillState, 127, Onsu-dong, Guro-gu, Seoul, Korea

버닝 썬

태양이 불탄다
지난여름의 폭염에
지구가 녹아내릴 듯 숨막혔는데
얼마나 더 뜨겁기에
태양마저 삼키려는가

허리우드 액션 어드벤쳐의
영화제목이 아니다

사회 상층부 강남의 남성권력과
폭력의 실체가 도사리는 곳

불타는 청춘의 욕망이 빚은
가학적 증상을
우린 버닝 썬이라고 명명한다.

* 버닝썬 : 강남의 유흥주점 이름

PANATENEAS
("Amor d'un ombra e gelosia d'un aura")
DOMENICO SCARLATTI

Waltz of roses dance the violet afternoon,
to the fugitive sound to the bassoonist?s wind.
The great forest exhales its fragrants breath.
A chorus of birds essays its operetta...

The landscape is impressed by the paddle
of a terse lake ful of enchantment...
("What did your erotie feeling want
while your poet madrigalized")

In a fascinating ballet of reflexes
a red twilight arrived from far away
with its cheerful round of blonde stars...

And(while drunk I enjoyed the delicacies
of your unpolluted and untouched purecies)
the moon admired your alabasters!

Mario Ruiz de Castilla/Peru

Alameda Bolognesi No. 706,
Quinta "La Tartaria"
Ciudad de Ayacucho, PERU, South America.

진분홍 제비꽃

제비꽃 핀 오후에, 장미의 왈츠가
관악기 바람의 사라지는 소리에 맞춰 춤춘다.
위대한 숲은 그 향기로운 숨을 쉰다.
새들의 합창은 그 가희극을 상연하고…….

풍경은 매혹으로 가득한 작은 호수의
보트 위에 있는 노에 의해 감명 지어 진다.
(너의 시가 연주 되는 동안
너의 애정어린 감정은 무엇을 원하는가?)

그림자로 비치는 환상적인 무용처럼
빨간 빛은 즐거운 금빛의 별과 함께
멀리서 쏟아져 온다.

그리고(술 마시는 동안 나는
너의 오염되지 않고, 손닿지 않은 순수의 기막힘을 즐긴다)
달은 너의 눈꽃 같은 모습을 찬미하노라!

Alice Goldmann

Safely at rest her alabaster features
serene and self-immersed, beyond the world,
she lay, my first and last of piano teachers,
from yester night into forever hurled.
Her trembling lover, founts of passion streaming,
with tears his shaky conscience to restore,
her mute resolve through years of silcence screaming
the tuneless parting words of Never more.
The melodies that I could never master,
like uncreated souls awaiting birth,
keep crowding on my soul and circling faster
in eddies swallowed by the whirl-pool's girth.

Now, after sixth years, her presence rises
to meet me at the gate of no return
and memory, as I approach it, prizes
her spirit that sought refuge in an urm.

Eric Vio / Portugal

Casa da Rampa,
Malveira da Serra,
Cascais,
2750 Portugal

내 사랑 앨리스

편안하게 휴식중인 그녀의 희고 매끄러운 모습은
속세를 초월한 청아하고, 자기 몰입된 자태.
나의 첫 번째며 마지막 피아노 선생인 그녀는
어젯밤에서 영원에까지 허공에 누워 있다.
흐르는 열정의 샘인 그녀의 애인은
눈물로 그의 흔들리는 양심을 되찾았고
그녀의 침묵은 울부짖는 침묵의 세월을 통해
더 이상은 없을 곡조 없는 이별의 말을 치유한다.
탄생을 기다리는 창조되지 않은 영혼처럼
내가 이해할 수 없는 노랫가락이
나의 영혼 위에 구름져 있으며
회오리 중심에 의해 삼켜지는
소용돌이처럼 빠르게 휘돌아 온다.

그 육십년 후인 지금, 그녀의 존재는
돌아올 수 없는 문과 기억 속에서
나를 만나러 일어서며, 가까이 갈수록
나는 묘 속에서 안식처를 찾지 못하는
그녀 영혼을 소중히 한다.

My Name

My name
I was told since I was very little
means "felicidad"
You should be happy, sabes?
We come to live on Earth!
Our body
produces a few flowers
as the herbs do.
Happiness: "Felicidad"
a star for us.

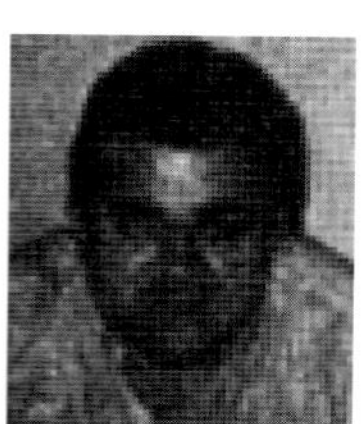

Daniel De Culla/Spain

POBox 2117
09080-Burgos-Spain

나의 이름

내가 아주 어렸을 적부터
들어오던 나의 이름은
너는 행복해야 한다는 뜻의
"felicidad"를 의미한다.
우리는 지구 위에 살기 위해 오지 않았던가!
우리의 육체는
숲이 그러듯이
조금의 꽃들을 만들어낸다.
행복, 그 이름 "felicidad"
별이 우릴 위해 있다.

GALLOWS OVER EUROPE

Hand holds hand within hand,
It seems on need go nowhere,
And when the hands will need to part,
Let us hurry to die in one another.

My senses awake before the dawn:
I love you, I do.
With a heavy mouth day pants in demons of darkness,
There is no ray of light, nor can dawn's path be seen.
I love you, I do.
So complete, alone, without questions or galaxies of words,
I am space itself, borm from the glittering of love-
And, before my eyelids open I can notice
How the heaven of your eyes carries mine within them.
I love you, I do.

- Translated by Robert Fearnley

Andrejs Eglitis/Sweden

Latvian National Foundation
Lettiska Nationella Fonden
101021 Stockholm 1
Box 108, Sweden

유럽 위의 교수대

손안에서 손이 손을 잡고 있다.
그것은 아무데도 갈곳이 필요없는 듯 하다.
그리고 손과 손이 이별을 필요로 할 때
우린 서로 죽음을 재촉하자.

나의 감각은 새벽 전에 깨어난다.
나는 너를 사랑한다. 정말 사랑한다.
무거운 입으로 낮은 어둠의 귀신 속에서 헐떡인가.
빛의 방사도 없고 새벽길도 보일 수 없다.
나는 사랑한다. 정말 사랑한다.
그렇게 완전하게, 혼자 말의 은하수도 질문도 없이
나는 사랑의 반짝임에서 태어난 우주 그 자체다.
나는 어떻게 너의 눈의 하늘이 그들 속으로 나를
데려 가는 지를 볼 수 있다.
나는 사랑한다. 정말 사랑한다.

THE SOUL CONTENT

A youth can find no place on earth today
Without a body exquisitely made
From liquid ores and metals that pervade
The ocean water flowing round a cay
Of granite rock irradiate with spray;
Where storms and torrents endlessly have flayed
From out the living stone, in sun and shade,
The breath of life and souls from brine and clay:
With love his place upon the earth is sure,
When to his yearning flesh warm hope is lent-
For pain and hardships that he must endure-
By those who love and give his aims consent,
Who know that faith forever can insure
Against all harm and leave the soul content.

Eleanor Otto / U.S.A

400 W. 43St., Apt. 27-T
New York, New York 10036
U.S.A.

영혼의 만족

바다는 분말로 방사하는
화강암의 둥근 만을 때린다.
젊음은 바다를 스미는 유동성철과 금속으로
만들어진 육체없인 지구위에 설 곳이 없다.
폭풍과 격류가 끝없이 살아 있는 바위로부터
껍질을 벗는 곳, 그 태양과 해변에서
삶은 숨쉬고 영혼은 소금물과 점토에서 방황한다.
사랑. 그의 지구위의 위치는 확실하고
그의 갈망하는 육체에 따스한 희망이 붙을 때……
그가 견뎌야 하는 고난과 고통을 위해……
사랑하고 목표를 일치시키는 사람과
믿음은 모든 악에 대항해 영원이 존재한다는 말을
그때야 영혼은 만족한다.

If We Want go to Come

The Time is Now we Have to Act
If we Want God to Come.

Can You Imagine Seeing God
And His Trillion Angel Sons.
The Bells Will Tool The World Rejoice
Each Face Will Look Above-

Up to The King of Kings;
Lord of Lords-Stunned!

This Time He'll Wear no Crown of Thorns
Instead a Crown of-Gold!
Before This Great Event Takes Place
His Word we Shall Unfold-His Good News-
Unite-Humanity Come Together as One-

Grace Galasso St.Dawn / U.S.A

340 Elliot Place
Paramus, N.J. 07652
U.S.A.

만약 신이 오길 바란다면

지금은 우리가 행동해야 할 시간
만약 신이 오길 바란다면

신과 수많은 천사 아들들을 보는 것을
상상할 수 있는가?
종은 울릴 것이다－세상은 기뻐하고
모든 얼굴은 위를 볼 것이다.
왕중의 왕까지
군주중의 군주까지－기절시킬 것이다
지금 그는 금왕관 대신 가시왕관을 쓰지 않을 것이다.
이 거대한 사건이 일어나기 이전
우리는 그의 좋은 소식을 밝힐 것이다
일치와 인간성은 하나로서 함께 온다는 것을

만약 신이 오길 바란다면.

The Stars

The stars do not deceive us. Only we
trouble them with our probings. They are not
apple's, bobbing in a witch's pot,
ready for biting; but buoys in a cosmic sea
of rolling infinity. Set to measure time
in atom or solar system, small or great,
they tell us symmetry is all. Their light
invites men to partake of heaven's dream.

Study each star, then kneel and pray; for you
and I, as they, will orbit the sun, and die;
but planets never lie. They tell it true
making their faithful stations in the sky.
God shows us, erratic men, their patterned ways
that we may see the order of His Grace.

Hyacinthe Hill/U. S. A.

c/o Scop & Gleeman
876 Las Ovejas
San Rafael, CA 94903

별들

별들은 우리를 속이지 않는다. 단지 우리만이
그들을 조사함으로써 괴롭힌다. 그들은
마녀의 항아리 속에서 움직이며 깨물려 하는
사과도 아니다. 그러나 단지 회전하는 우주의
무한성의 바다에 있는 부표이다.
작은 원자나 큰 태양계 내에서 시간을 재기 위해서
그들이 우리에게 말하는 것은 균형이 전부이다. 그들의 빛은
인간을, 하늘의 꿈을 나누도록 초대한다.

모든 별을 연구하고 무릎을 꿇고 기도하라. 그대와
나를 위하여, 그들이 태양을 공전하고 죽는 것처럼, 그러나
행성은 결코 거짓말 하지 않는다. 그들은 하늘에서
그들의 믿음직스런 주장을 하는데 있어 진실을 말한다.
신은 변덕스런 우리에게 그의 자비의 질서를
볼 수 있도록 정해진 길을 보여준다.

Songs of Wonder

Olympic games date back to ancient times
When Greek contestants vied with varied skills,
Where great festivities brought sporting thrills
And celebrations fraught with metric rhymes.

Once more, to celetial heights the victor climbs;
Magestic music drifts through distant hills
And laurel crowns are worn with pride that fills
Rejoicing hearts... like Zeus's wind-blown chimes.

Congratulations to Professor Sam,
A glorious leader of the written word,
For his anthologies of lyric verse
And for the linking, yea, the cryptogram
Of peace which, not unlike the singing bird,
Brings exaltation to the universe.

Vivian Way Bonine, A.L.D./U.S.A.

- Address : 2556 La Presa Avenue Rosemead CA 91770 U.S.A.

경탄의 노래

올림픽 경기는 고대로 거슬러 간다.
그리스의 경쟁자들이 다양한 기술로 겨루던 때,
위대한 축제가 운동가의 오싹한 전율과
운율로 가득한 찬양을 가져온 곳.

이제 다시, 천국 높은 곳까지 승리가 울려 퍼지리니;
장엄한 음악이 멀리 언덕들에까지 뻗어가고
즐거운 마음을 가득 채운 자긍심으로
월계관은 씌워진다. 마치 제우스의, 바람에 날리는 종소리처럼

Sam 교수님에게 축하를,
영광스런 단어의 선도자이신,
그의 서정 명시선집을 위해
그리고 결합 즉
노래하는 새와 다름없이
우주에 환희를 가져다 주는
평화의 암호를 위해.

Mother's Mind

When she opens the cover of a kettle
With her white hairs flapping,
The mother's face blooming like steam
Is still beautiful.

Early morning
She crosses herself with a rice scoop
On the rice food she made newly,
And prayed for one day of her daughter.

Park In-ae / U.S.A

*Debut as a poet through 『The Literary Movement & Trend』 "Korea Association of Elite Essayists"
*Debut as a novelist through 『The Seoulmunhakin』
*Member of the Korean Writers' Association
*Director of the Korean Literature Society of America
*Director of the World Poetry Research Institute
*The 5th President of Korean Literature Society of Dallas & now Councilwoman
*Graduate of Kyung Hee Cyber University, E-learning Course on Creative Writing
*A Staff Editor of The Third Literature in America
*Instructor of Korean Literature Class in Culture Center of the Jungang Daily New's Paper
*Columnist for the 'News Korea' a weekly news magazine.
*The 29th Great Prize of the world Poetry
*Won the Prize of the 26th Korea Literature Abroad
*Essay collection book 『Chattering and Speaking Out』 published by The Third Literature
*In-Ae Park, Comes Across the Magic Flower
*Author Poetry book 『Coloring the Wind』 published by The Third Literature
*Languages Swallow Laguages, and Words Draw Words, etc.
*Resides in 11528 HARRY HINES BLVD #A-116 DALLAS, TX 75229 U.S.A
*Contact email: nadainae@naver.com

The daughter who ate the rice food her mother prayed on
And grew up, scoops rice out of the pot for her daughter.
She crosses herself on the steam rising rice food,
Fills a bowl of prayer.

Another day
I see her daughter stop abruptly
To scoop rice out before a kettle
And also see her daughter' s eyelid turning red.

- Tr. by Won Eung-Soon

어머니 마음

밥솥 뚜껑을 열면
흰머리 날리며
김처럼 피어오르는 어머니 모습
아직도 곱다

이른 아침
갓 지은 밥 위에
주걱으로 십자가를 그리며
자식의 하루를
기도하셨던 어머니

기도 밥 먹고 자란 딸이
자식 위해 밥을 푼다
김이 오르는 밥 위에
십자가를 긋고
기도 한 그릇 담는다

먼 훗날
밥솥 앞에서 밥 푸다 말고
멈칫 선 딸아이가 보인다
그 아이 눈시울이 붉다

世界詩文學會 沿革 History of The Society of the World Poetry

- 1982. 11. 26 세계시문학회 창립총회 초대회장 김영삼 시인
- 1982 ~1993 정기총회(매년 상반기)
- 1994 6. 27 세계시문학회 제2대 회장 김정웅 시인
- 1994 ~2012 정기총회(매년 상반기)
- 1998. 12. 5 제16집 세계시문학 출판기념회 및 제12회 가야금관왕관상 시상식
- 1999. 11. 27 제17집 세계시문학 출판기념회 및 제13회 가야금관왕관상 시상식

⋮

- 2013. 10. 4 세계시문학회 제3대 회장 정송전 시인
- 2013. 11. 29 제31집 세계시문학 출판기념회 및 제27회 가야금관왕관상 시상식
- 2014. 4.1~2 세계시문학회 제32차 세미나
- 2014. 6. 24 세계시문학회 제4대 회장 원응순 시인
- 2014. 12. 18 제32집 세계시문학 출판기념회 및 제28회 세계시문학상 시상식
- 2015. 11. 24 제33집 세계시문학 출판기념회 및 제29회 세계시문학상 시상식
- 2016. 3. 31~4. 1 문학기행 및 시낭송회(전남 순천 · 구례 일원)
- 2016. 10. 26 한 · 중 시문학 세미나 및 시화전(2016. 10. 15~11. 20)
- 2016. 11. 29 제34집 세계시문학 출판기념회 및 제30회 세계시문학상 시상식
- 2017. 2. 21 제36차 정기총회
- 2017. 3. 23 확대 임원회의 및 이사 추대식
- 2017. 4. 25 문학기행 및 시낭송회(경기도 여주 일원)
- 2017. 9. 1 유관순시단과 함께하는 시낭송회
- 2017. 10. 14 난빛축제와 함께하는 시낭송회
- 2017. 11. 28 제35집 세계시문학 출판기념회 및 제31회 세계시문학상 시상식
- 2018. 2. 20 제37차 정기총회
- 2018. 4. 27 문학기행 (충남 당진 심훈문학관 일대)
- 2018. 6. 26 임원회의 및 이사 추대식
- 2018. 10. 20 난빛축제와 함께하는 시화전
- 2018. 11. 23 제36집 세계시문학 출판기념회 및 제32회 세계시문학상 시상식
- 2019. 2. 19 제 38차 정기총회－합정동 들풀
- 2019. 3. 26 세계시문학회 제6대 회장 오진환 시인
회장 이 취임식 및 임원 · 이사 위촉식
- 2019. 4. 23 봄 문학기행－강원도 양구, 두타연, 평화의 댐 일원
- 2019. 6. 3~7 라오스 해외 문학 연수－동독국립대학교, 비엔티안, 방비엥 일원
- 2019. 9. 24 시낭송회－인사동 시가연
- 2019. 10. 24 가을 문학기행－충북 소월 · 경암 문학기념관 방문 후
수안보파크호텔 알프스홀에서 문학특강 및 시낭송회 가짐.

Winners of KAYA Golden Crown World Poets Award

Year	Country	Name of Winners
1986	KOREA	KIM IL-RO
1987	KOREA	LEE HAN-HO
〃	U.S.A.	ROSEMARY C.WILKINSON
1988	U.S.A.	VICTORY OURINE
〃	KOREA	MOON DEOK-SOO
〃	C. I. S.(RUSSIA)	DOLMA TOVSKY EUGINE
〃	ESPANA	TOMAS BEVIA ARANDA
〃	INDIA	D.K.JOY
1989	KOREA	SHIN DONG-JIP
〃	U.S.A.	ELLIS OVESEN
〃	YUGO(Sarajevo)	DR. AJSA ZAHIROVIC
〃	KOREA	JEONG KI-SEOK
1990	U.S.A.	DR. MARY J. BANERS
〃	KOREA	DR. KIM DONG-NI
〃	KOREA	DR. YUN JONG-HYOK
1991	JAPAN	UEMOTO MASAO
〃	KOREA	LIM JI-HYUN
〃	AUSTRALIA	JOY BEAUDETTE CRIPS
〃	KOREA	LIM HEON-DO
1992	KOREA	BAEK HAN-YI

Year	Country	Name of Winners
1992	BRAZIL	ANGELA MARIA ROCHA BIASE
〃	KOREA	YANG SANG-WOOK
〃	CHINA P.R.	CHEN-HUI JIN
1993	KOREA	KIM JI-HYANG
〃	ISRAEL	ADA AHARONI
〃	JAPAN	JUNKO HAMAE
〃	KOREA	DR. KIM JOUNG-WOONG
〃	CHINA P.R.	Prof. LU JIN
1994	KOREA	CHOI YUN-YOUNG
1995	KOREA	LEE CHANG-HWAN
1996	KOREA	SON KI-SUB
1997	KOREA	KIM MIN-SEONG
1998	KOREA	KIM NAM-WOONG
〃	KOREA	KIM CHUI-KYONG
1999	KOREA	LEE JAE-HYUN
〃	KOREA	JUNG SOON-YOUNG
〃	KOREA	PARK KEUN-HOO
2000	KOREA	JIN EUL-JU
〃	CHINA	GE NAI FU
2001	KOREA	LEE KI-BAN
2002	JAPAN	JUN UENO

Year	Country	Name of Winners
2003	KOREA	KIM CHANG-JIK
〃	KOREA	KIM JI-WON
2004	JAPAN	NATIKO WATANABE
〃	KOREA	CHUNG OK-IN
2005	KOREA	SEO JEONG-NAM
〃	KOREA	LEE JI-YOUNG
〃	KOREA	JUNG U-HA
2006	KOREA	OH MIN-PHIL
〃	KOREA	KIM SUNG-YOUL
〃	KOREA	LEE JONG-IL
2007	KOREA	SHIN SOON-AE
〃	KOREA	CHO KI-HYUN
2008	KOREA	CHOI SEUNG-BEOM
〃	KOREA	KANG HAE-KUN
2009	KOREA	SHIN DONG-MYEUNG
〃	KOREA	KIM JONG-WON
2010	KOREA	PARK MOON-JAE
〃	KOREA	LIM WON-SIK
〃	KOREA	EUN YO-SUK
2011	KOREA	KIM KYE-YOON
〃	KOREA	KIM IL-RYE
2012	KOREA	CHOUNG SONG-JUN
〃	KOREA	JIN SANG-SOON
〃	KOREA	NO JUNG-AI

Year	Country	Name of Winners
2013	KOREA	JUN DUK-KI
〃	KOREA	JUNG SUN-JA
〃	KOREA	OH JIN-HWAN
〃	KOREA	KOU SUN-JA
2014	KOREA	KIM KYEONG-SOON
〃	KOREA	KIM DON-YOUNG
〃	KOREA	LEE JAE-HO
〃	KOREA	LEE SEOK-GI
2015	KOREA	KO BANG-KYU
〃	KOREA	PARK IN-AE
〃	KOREA	LEE BYUNG-SEOK
〃	KOREA	WEE MAENG-RYANG
2016	KOREA	JANG DONG-SUCK
〃	KOREA	BANG JUNG-SUN
〃	KOREA	LEE SU-JEONG
2017	KOREA	KIM JONG-HEE
〃	KOREA	PARK YOUN-KI
〃	KOREA	KANG YOUNG-DUK
2018	KOREA	HONG YUN-PYEO
〃	KOREA	JEON HONG-GU
2019	KOREA	KIM JEONG-WON
〃	KOREA	JUNG HYUN-IM
〃	KOREA	YOON HYOUNG-SOON

세계시문학회 조직

The system of the Society of the World Poetry

세계시문학 제37집(2019)

인쇄 2019년 11월 20일
발행 2019년 11월 27일

발행인 오진환
편집주간 김효열
편집위원 신동명 맹숙영 윤수아 김돈영

발행처 **세계시문학회**
주소 서울시 마포구 양화진길41, 일신오피스텔 603호
전자우편 **wp1982@hanmail.net**
우편번호 04083

제작처 **을지출판공사**
전화 02) 334-4050 팩시밀리 02) 334-4010

값 20,000원

ISBN 978-89-7566-183-9 03810

세계시문학회 계좌번호

농협 301-0246-6480-91 세계시문학회(오진환)